Ploughing the Home Ground

Ploughing the Home Ground

Essays on Canadian Literature and Poetics

Don Gutteridge

First Edition

QuodSermo Publishing
www.HiddenBrookPress.com
QuodSermo@gmail.com

Title: Ploughing the Home Ground
Author: Don Gutteridge

Cover Design – Richard M. Grove
Layout and Design – Richard M. Grove
Cover Image – Red maple leaves in Autumn
by Stephen Chang,
by permission Shutterstock Canada

Typeset in Garamond
Printed and bound in Canada

Library and Archives Canada Cataloguing in Publication

Title: Ploughing the home ground : essays on Canadian literature and poetics / Don Gutteridge.
Names: Gutteridge, Don, 1937- author.
Description: First edition. |
Series statement: CanLit revealed
Identifiers: Canadiana (print) 2021036582X |
Canadiana (ebook) 20210365846 |
ISBN 9781989786598 (softcover) |
ISBN 9781989786604 (ebook)
Subjects: LCSH: Canadian literature—History and criticism.
Classification: LCC PS8061 .G88 2021 |
DDC C810.9—dc23

This book is dedicated

to CanLit,

to the writers,

the editors,

the publishers,

and to the readers.

Contents

Preface

This little book is a collection of some of the essays and review articles (and ordinary reviews that got out-of-hand) that I started writing some 60 years ago. While each of them was incited by a specific event, a timely request, or an urgent question in my on-going literary life, they do attain – collectively – a certain focus and coherence. This is probably due to the simple fact that they deal with the commonplace, but irresolvable, issues which beset most writers of fiction and poetry in any age. Questions about *how* poems get made soon get re-cast, in a neophyte nation like Canada, to include *why* they get made. Such questions are timeless. The matter of the relationship between writer and reader gets further complicated by regional-centralist tensions with their eccentric, bi-focal, ironic character. Hence, questions of poetics and of the politics of interpretation intersect easily, and take on – from the writer's perspective – a continuing and jarring urgency. It is in this light and from this angle that these occasional pieces ought to be read.

The selections have been arranged in chronological order of their first publication, in part to give the reader a chance to see these urgencies and my corresponding enthusiasms played out over time – with all the resultant inconsistency and unevenness of development.

While tempted to expunge all infelicities and other blemishes, I have left the selections pretty much as they originally appeared. Only the piece on "Riel" has been edited, as it was originally a dramatized talk. Minor errors of fact have been corrected; and aspects of formatting and referencing have been altered for the sake of consistency.

I would like to thank the editors of the journals who published these essays and otherwise encouraged me to continue writing them; in particular, Denis Smith, Dennis Cooley, the late Geoffrey Milburn and Fred Cogswell, Stan Dragland, and W.H. New. My gratitude is also extended to those colleagues who over the years and often unwittingly have helped me shape and sharpen my arguments: R D Gidney, Robin Barrow, Robin Mathews, the late Colm O'Sullivan, and Ian Underhill.

Acknowledgements

The essays in this collection appeared originally in these Canadian periodicals:

- *The Bulletin of the Canadian Humanities Association* ("Riel: Historical Man or Literary Symbol?")
- *The Journal of Canadian Studies* ("Teaching the Canadian Mythology" and "Surviving the Fittest")
- *The History and Social Science Teacher* ("History as Public and Private Metaphor" and "Regions of the Heart")
- *Contemporary Verse II* ("Local Colour, Communal Consciousness, and Loretta Lynn")
- *Brick* ("Homage to the Past-Future")
- *The English Quarterly* ("The Coherence of Consonance in Poetry")
- *Canadian Literature* ("Local Culture and the National Will" and "Old Photographs and the Documentary Imperative")
- *Canadian Forum* (" Surfacing")

Riel: Historical Man or Literary Symbol?

1

For a long time now I have been interested in the problems of adapting historical materials for literary purposes, and felt that I might make use of my recent experience in writing *Riel: A Poem for Voices* to develop and clarify some ideas which have lain half-formed in my mind for the last nine years. Before beginning, I feel compelled to preface my remarks with two disclaimers. First of all, I am not a historian, either by training or inclination, and so I beg your indulgence if I presume to remark too boldly upon historiographical matters. Secondly, I am not a literary scholar, though I occasionally confess to have had some training along that line. I am, however, going to discuss – with the temerity of all foolish angels who rush blindly in – both history and literature. I do so with the only authority to which I can honestly lay any claim: that of a poet, who for the last nine years has been writing, and sometimes publishing, poems which are rooted in history – specifically the history of this country. But more of that later.

Let me begin with a recent, barbarous review that appeared in *Edge* magazine, and was penned by one Edward A. Lacey, pseudonym. As will be soon apparent, I made the grossest error in writing a short preface to the poem, in which I said, "In an attempt to come to grips with the current French-English problem *in poetic terms*, I turned to the history of Louis Riel." It seems to me, in retrospect, that it was a misreading of this statement which led Mr. Lacey, our pseudonymous reviewer, to make such remarks as the following:

Several of the books I shall be reviewing here are from the poisoned crop of 1967, and some of these poets are Luddites, and obviously do care about Canada and what happens to it, and one must examine their works in the light of their beliefs. The first such volume to come to hand is a curious antiquity by Don Gutteridge, *Riel: A Poem for Voices* (Fiddlehead Books, 1968, 52 pp), a long four-part dramatic poem, presumably meant for radio recitation, consisting of monologues delivered by the individual dramatic personae, relieved and mixed with "voices," basically choral interludes which range from letters, newspaper advertisements, accounts and editorials relevant to the events of Riel's life and death, to Indian chants.

I must quarrel with Mr. Gutteridge's basic premise (which of course doesn't affect the poem's artistic validity), that his poem is an attempt to come to grips with the French-English problem in poetic terms. The French-Canadians are not, and were not, the same thing as the Indians, by a long shot. Even though the WASP attitude toward the two groups may have been basically the same (and this is highly disputable), the groups' concept of, and attitude to, themselves, were very different.[1]

At this point he goes on, quite rightly, to show that the historical situation now is radically different from that of one hundred years ago. However, he has missed the essential point here, for I was attempting to reveal in *poetic*, not historical, terms the relationship between Riel's story and our present racial problems. I knew perfectly well when I began writing *Riel* that Metis were not French Canadians, and that Manitoba and Saskatchewan were not Quebec. But Mr. Lacey has assumed that I was writing a poeticized form of history, when I was actually writing historically based poetry, or poetry in which historical data provides an essential source of metaphor and symbol. In short, Mr. Lacey has raised – unintentionally perhaps – the problem of the relationship between literature and history. What is poetry? and what is history? And what in the world are they when one encounters them together in unholy wedlock? Can Louis Riel be simultaneously historical man and literary symbol?

Our pseudonymous reviewer brings yet another charge against me in regard to my handling of history:

Recognising, then, that Riel is about the subculture we have destroyed, not the one we are at present destroying, I have one further complaint – the evident bias with which Mr. Gutteridge treats Riel's opponents and mingles fancy with history. The quotation from Alexander Henry shocks with its horror and authenticity, the lengthy excerpts from *The Globe and Mail* sadden one with their reminder of what Ontarians are, and were, and the discreditable part they played in the events under discussion, and the sensitive and poetic rearrangements of Riel's address to the court and of the recorded comments of bystanders at his execution bring the poem to a moving conclusion. But what of Dr. Schultz's monologue and self-portrait, and especially the pseudo-quotation from Thomas Scott? What is Mr. Gutteridge's authority for considering Scott a sadist to animals (except, of course, Canadian cultural traditions) or for causing him to speak an unauthentic, sub-literate garble. I'd similarly challenge the shrinking-violet letter which a soldier in the first Riel campaign reportedly writes home to his father – the tone doesn't ring true. If Mr. Gutteridge is going to invent material, let him do so credibly. Apart from these instances, though, our author seems to have done his research and his combining and selecting of material well.[21]

I stand accused here of mingling "fancy with history" and of bringing to the poem an "evident bias". Both accusations imply that Mr. Lacey has come to the poem as if it were poetic history, and his complaints would be perfectly valid if the poem were indeed such an animal. It is not. It is simply a poem with history as its organizing metaphor. Also, I would assume that most readers go to poetry precisely because it *does* have a kind of bias, a bias which in its own way might provide us with insight not only into history but into the human condition regardless of its historical setting. Mr. Lacey also charges that some of the invented material is not "credible". If he means that these sections are not true to the poem, then I accept this criticism with reluctant good grace. If, however, he means that they lack historical credibility, (and I suspect he does, considering the context of his remarks) then we are back to the basic problem once again: is this history or poetry? And if it is both, then how do we come to grips with the combination in critical and responsive terms?

It seems to me that there are two basic questions raised here by Mr. Lacey. 1) What is the difference between poetic history and historical poetry, and 2) regardless of these differences, what kind of bias is permissible in a poem with historical overtones, and how do we learn to "read" it so that it has some valid meaning for us? In short, what is the nature of its validity?

It is these two questions upon which I hope to shed some tenuous and tentative light. As a non-scholar and non-historian I can only hope to do so by explaining to you what my intentions were, and how I proceeded to handle my source materials. Perhaps these honest confessions of the man who made the poem may be of some use both to the historian who wishes, somehow, to include literary materials as part of his intellectual framework, and to the literary man who, day in and day out, brings his mind and emotions to the raw stuff of literature: the poem.

2

I will attempt at this point to make some sweeping generalizations about the difference between poetic history and historical poetry – not because they will hold true under close scrutiny nor absolutely define an area whose edges in reality are almost always blurred, but because it is through a longer perspective that we might be able to discern what is really going on in the historical poem. Speaking cautiously, we can define two basic kinds of literary/historical materials. In the first kind, which might be labelled *poeticized history*, the purpose is to make history "come alive", as it were, by rendering it in the more accessible forms of literature. I am thinking here primarily of the so-called historical novel, like *The Viking* by Mika Waltari or *Sword at Sunset* by Rosemary Sutcliff. The former tries to give the reader a sense of the Viking period, and while the story-line is mostly invented, there is accurate attention given to descriptive detail dealing with people, places, and events of that historical time. In the Sutcliff novel, the reader is plunged into the world of King Arthur (called Artos the Bear in the book). The story may be legendary, but we come face to face with such historical figures as the Saxons, Hengest and Horsa, and leave the book quite convinced that Miss Sutcliff has done her homework well, for not only the characters, but the landscape, the Romanized towns and the particular kind of warfare of that period are described with loving care.

Nevertheless, I feel that anyone who did a thorough study of this kind of book would soon discover that the lines between history and literature are not always clearly drawn. For example, Waltari's book is written in the romance mode, and one senses the shaping presence of the mode throughout, especially its insistence on a Hollywood-type love story. We may have accurate historical data in varying degrees in many historical novels, but the literary person is also aware of the exigencies of the literary mode working to shape the materials into a novel (or play or poem). The point I wish to make here is that even in the commonly accepted form of historical novel, or drama (like *Elizabeth the Queen*) or poem (like *Brébeuf and his Brethren*), there are problems presented which involve the subtle relationship between literary mode/genre and the historical materials which can be utilized in a variety of ways. This complex problem is perhaps best illustrated by Dickens' *A Tale of Two Cities*, for here we have not only the typical use of historical setting and event, superimposed on the typical romantic plot with typically romanticized characters, but we must also face the fact that the book purports to elaborate and justify Carlyle's rather misguided historiographical view of the French Revolution.

However it is the second kind of historical/literary combination with which as a poet I am here concerned. In this type, the writer – most likely a poet or dramatist – uses the historical materials as symbol or structuring principle in order to make a personal statement of his own or, put another way and more pompously, to reveal the universal in the particular. This point is often misunderstood in dealing with historically based literature of this kind. Here the poet uses history in the same way that he might use nature imagery, psychological theories, philosophical ideas, sociological trends, etc. – all are part of a common and shared knowledge, and thus are raw material for the poet's neurotic obsession with symbol-making. Keats, for example, used the nightingale in its conventional setting, not because he was a bird-lover, but because he saw in the bird the possibility of rendering a certain mood and a complex set of emotions and thoughts. This is not to say that a poet selects such materials arbitrarily, for it is precisely because he can *feel* the potential meaning in his referents, as symbol and as object, that he can create valid poetry. In fact, one of the difficulties in discriminating between poets and pseudo-poets is often centred on this point: do the symbols operate on us in a merely academic or intellective way, or do they convince us of their validity both as symbols and as recognizable objects? To read "Ode to a Nightingale" is to relive the actual experiences of Keats. We are there with him in that garden, hearing that nightingale, following the poet's mind back into the magic landscape drawn for us in stanzas four and five, and on to Ruth "amid the alien corn", and back out to the cold reality of the tolling bell and the English hillside. Whatever the poem eventually comes to mean for us, its essential hold over the mind and feelings derives from the fact that its images and symbols are referents to a whole experience which we recognize or are brought to recognize. This is not to say that the best poets must use only the familiar landscape to convince us. Keats, for example, in "La Belle Dame Sans Merci", creates a nightmare landscape of his own making, but the individual objects within that landscape are vividly rendered: the withered sedge, the songless woods, the cold hillside, the dismayed knight, and the lady with the wild, wild eyes – all these are referents to parts of a reality which we recognize, and they become, in the forge of the poem itself, part of a larger reality which emanated from Keat's own imaginative needs. Again, we are compelled to live through a strange and yet utterly convincing experience.

Much of the foregoing is common knowledge to those who deal with poetry in their daily lives, and we have come to accept the use of landscape, seasons, even myth, as respectable source material for literature. However, when writers use *historical* materials in the same way, they are often mis-read. For some writers (not all) historical events and personages hold the same kind of imaginative potential as nightingales or medieval romance did for Keats. They find in history a ready source of symbol or structure for their work, and quite often have a rather cavalier concern for history in any sense that would please an historian. The unsuspecting reader may go to such poems, plays, or novels expecting to find interpretive history and be justifiably disappointed.

Why, then, would a poet who wished to write a long poem on an heroic person select an historical figure of such prominence as Riel, one who has stirred so much controversy and partisan argument, if he does not intend to interpret these events in some way that might be construed as historical? Would it not be more judicious to invent a wholly fictitious character who might serve his purposes equally well, and at the same time avoid the controversial and historiographical entanglements generated by any attempt to deal with Louis Riel? One answer, of course, is that this approach is perfectly feasible, and is often used by poets and others. But this answer, quite simply, will not do for me (nor I suspect for Pratt in *The Titanic*, Shaw in *St. Joan*, or Bolt in *A Man for All Seasons*). It will not do for me because in the last nine years [1960-1969] I have written long poems on figures from Canadian history like Dollard, Brébeuf, Hudson, Champlain, La Salle, and Louis Riel. Although I've spent most of a decade writing poems about historical figures and events, I have only recently paused long enough to ask myself *why*. What follows is a tentative attempt to answer this question and the others which I raised earlier: what is historical poetry and wherein lies its validity?

3

First, I have always wanted to write what Archibald MacLeish has called poetry of the public world, i.e., poetry whose symbols and referents would be part of the common wisdom of Canadian readers – not because I am a nationalist, but because I am hopelessly a Canadian, having been born, raised, educated, and professionally turned out in an area not more than sixty miles in diameter, whose centre happens to be London, Ontario. This desire to write public poetry is no doubt due to the example of E.J. Pratt. Paradoxically, though, I discovered quite early that I was not E.J. Pratt reborn and refurbished, because all of my poetry turned out to be intensely personal and stubbornly private. Nevertheless, I continued to find that writing my own kind of narrative poem about historical figures was increasingly rewarding. I was, it seemed, writing private poems about public figures.

Secondly, I have always felt that there was an advantage in using symbolic material that was part of the common heritage. I now feel that there are two justifications for this view: 1) My own personal and psychological make-up required me to use elaborate Yeatsian masks through which I could safely explore my own troubled inner world, and 2) I wanted my poetry to have reference to me as an individual and to the past from which I evolved and by which I was involuntarily shaped. I suppose that is what MacLeish really meant by public poetry.

Thirdly, I discovered about the same time that I could write about only certain historical figures. My adolescent fantasies about composing the great Canadian epic soon collapsed about me when I found that I could not write a poem about William Lyon MacKenzie or Sir Guy Carleton (a teen-age idol of mine in those halcyon days before the Beatles and Bob Dylan) or, most regretfully, the Right Honourable John George Diefenbaker. In fact, I was drawn only to certain kinds of historical figures, whose "stories" provided me with those symbols and structures which could meet the demands made by my private need for expression.

From this brief autobiographical background we come to the present, and Louis Riel. For me, Riel was a natural extension of my original interest in men like La Salle and Champlain. His personality and story contained symbolic potential both for the private dilemmas I had been systematically exploring for seven years and for my desire to re-discover the peculiarly Canadian myths of my historical past. I fondly hoped that my readers would find meaning in my personal vision – for themselves as indivisible humans, and as Canadians who unintentionally happen to share a common mythology.

Before I discuss this vision and how its historical elements have become transmuted into poetry, I would like to refer you to the poem and the voice of Louis Riel, as he waits alone in Fort Garry for the arrival of Wolseley's army, and the disintegration of his dream:

Riel

And so, it had come to this: waiting for Wolseley
And his troops to assume form out of wilderness
Like black flies at the first heat, and not knowing.
He had *had* to kill Scott (would have done the same for
Boulton too, if the murdered boy's mother
Had not come like that, kneeling before him, her hands
Upon his, her lips shaping prayers that belonged
To another, to One great enough to forgive).

Scott had deserved death; for he was a symbol
Of all that stood in the way of their hopes, the vision:
Canadian, Orangeman, bigot, blasphemer,
A man without root, with no touch of the soil
In him or wind on him.

He'd voted death
With the others (four to three, his vote cancelling
Mercy), because the flowing inside was too strong,
Needed resistance of this rock to give it
Will and final direction (was *not* Scott's fists
There on the street, nor shame of eyes watching, *seeing*).
And yet, the soldiers *were* coming, and this earth
Would ripen with their bayonets. Could current
Be turned that easily? be blocked this close to sea?
Or could it carry some darkness of its own?
(Scott's blood a black coil on the innocent morning).
Outside, night gathered the rain unto itself
In a dark hoarding, and wind was an ancient plague
Settled around his house: black and wet, and awkward –
The cloak of a stranger.

The voice here is, I hope, poetry and not history, though the events referred to are historical facts. What makes this passage poetry (I trust) rather than history is its attempt to render the feelings of Louis Riel at this crucial moment in his life, and through this rendering to develop certain basic images which gather meaning as the poem progresses, and will become those kind of symbols that lift the poem from its historical moorings and raise it to the level of the universal. I want the reader to understand Louis Riel in this time and this place, to understand his attachment to the land and the revulsion he feels for those who do not share it with him, and to feel the images through which he habitually explores his own emotions and ideas: the flowing of currents, the wind as plague, man as a stranger in God's house – though the words and images are mine, I like to think that they might be historically probable or at least representative of what Riel would have thought. In this sense, then, the poem has historical validity of a certain kind. On the other hand, I am aware that there is as much of me in these lines as there is of the probable Louis Riel. (You will recall that Mr. Lacey referred to me as a Luddite, and I am, I guess.) To put this idea in other words, I found that I could render Riel's feelings because I conceived of them partly as my own. And it is precisely this symbiotic process which makes it possible to use history as symbol, to bring our vanished past not only into the perspective of the present (a task that many historians habitually perform), but also to draw that past into our own time through the consciousness of a single individual who uses not the intellectual rigours of the historian's trade, but his own deeply felt and fully realized identification with the people and events of our common past. And since I did not set out consciously to write poeticized history, the only validity that such a work might have – besides being a personal statement – is that I have found something in my own consciousness which is identical to that implied in Riel and his story. What this something is is not obviously a common environmental or temperamental experience – since I am not a Metis, do not speak French, am intractably presbyterian, and have no present plans to effect a revolution. Rather, it must be a commonality that runs more deeply in the human experience than event, or personality, or time and place. I have my own intuitions as to what this commonality is, having written the poem itself. Suffice it to say at this point that I am implying that a work of art which interprets historical events in the light of their symbolic or mythical meanings obtains any validity it might have by being "true" to its historical sources in the literary sense outlined above, and by being simultaneously "true" to the imaginative needs of its author at the time of writing. It is only when we really believe that these seemingly contradictory truths can be reconciled within the poem that literature can have any meaning for us.

4

Let me now illustrate what I mean by returning to Riel. I am briefly going to reconstruct the events which led to the writing of the poem, comment on the source materials I used, and demonstrate from the poem itself how historical fact, with some artistic manipulation, can become a symbolic statement which does not really violate history, but at the same time leaves history behind for something which may be more meaningful in human terms.

My first encounter with Louis Riel was quite accidental. It occurred while I was still at university. One evening I turned on the television set, and there I saw Louis Riel for the first time (actually it was Bruno Gerussi, who rendered a somewhat latinate version of our famous Metis rebel). The vehicle was John Coulter's *Louis Riel*, and I remember being fascinated by the play, the story, and the man. Shortly thereafter,

I read G.F. Stanley's standard biography of Riel, and then, gradually, the Riel story slipped to the back, or bottom, of my mind.

It was at least five years later, and after I had written three narrative poems, that I went to see an amateur production of the same Coulter play, performed at Althouse College of Education, with John Ferns in the title role. I felt that it was a superb performance of the play, but suddenly and certainly unexpectedly, I was unmoved by the play itself, by the very conception which it implied about Riel. And I remember feeling at the time that Coulter was not a native Canadian, and though he had researched his material thoroughly (much more thoroughly than I ever could, or would), he had missed what Riel really was in Canadian terms. He had got his history straight – for the play is faithful to the known and observable historical facts – but he had missed the meaning. And I do not mean here that he had failed to explain Louis Riel in a psychological sense (for there is little meaning to be found there), but simply that he had not seen or felt the essential conflict and the pervading tragedy of those important events from *our* past. The very fact that Coulter chose to use a chronicle form indicated to me that he was not prepared to see the story in poetic or mythical terms. And why should he? Indeed, how could he, not being a native Canadian (I mean here that he was not only not born here, but more seriously does not think or feel Canadian).

As I left the theatre that summer evening, I decided that the Riel story could best be rendered in some sort of poetic form, for somehow – I did not really know how, just then – the people and events seemed too large for the conventional stage, their meaning too complex for what I have called poeticized (or in this instance) dramatized history. Looking back on it now, I can see that it was my involvement with the problems of writing historical narrative poems which made me so unhappy with the same Coulter play which I had enjoyed a few years previously. At the same time I was becoming aware that Riel himself would be the culmination of my own work in this form. That evening I knew I would write a poem about Louis Riel.

Poets, however, are notoriously unorganized creatures. I suppose the normal procedure at this point was to dash to the nearest library and begin my research. In a sense, I did. But what emerged a few weeks later was a poem on Champlain. Yet another year passed, during which I was trying to exorcize the image of La Salle from my imagination (he's still there), and another narrative poem was written. Then in the fall of 1966, while browsing in a bookstore, I came upon *Strange Empire: the*

Story of Louis Riel by John Kinsey Howard, the American historian. From this moment on, there was no doubt that my next poem would be about Riel.

What was in Howard's account that I had not found in Stanley's biography or Coulter's play? Quite simply, it was imaginative, interpretive history, and lying dormant just below the vibrant surface of the book, those undeveloped symbols which my imagination had been seeking, in its own time and its own way, for two years. From an historian's viewpoint Howard and Stanley represent two historiographical polarities. Howard's book is interpretive, emotive, critical, beautifully written – what I would call a humanistic document. Stanley's biography is factual, well-documented, comprehensive – a reasonable and just account of Riel's life viewed largely from the outside through the rational eye of the trained historian. In my preface to the poem, I advise the reader to look at both these biographies if he wishes to get an historical perspective on the man and the period. From a poet's point of view, however, it is *Strange Empire* which attracts and holds the mind and the feelings. It may well be "bad history", perhaps because Howard seems to write the way a poet writes: selecting and arranging details to elucidate a pattern; describing people, events, even landscapes, in order to engage the reader's emotions; and finally working these individual parts together so that in total they make a human statement about our past – and in a sense, about ourselves who are necessarily implicated in our own history. Bernard de Voto in his preface to the book, sums it up this way:

Finally, the book is very fine art. The hope of a small company of writers is to bring history out of the seminar and restore it to the living room where it was once acknowledged to belong. Sacrificing none of the methods or the results of scholarship, they accept the heavy additional obligation of transforming scholarship into literature. That is what happens here. Everything in *Strange Empire* conforms absolutely to the discipline of fact but an equally disciplined historical imagination is at work, giving life to facts that would be dead without it and the craftsmanship put in its service. This is a drama of reality, not fantasy, of real men, not imagined ones, but the reader is led to participate in it as he might in the fictitious drama of the theatre – to the end that he may understand the deeds and the motives of men at a decisive hour. Tense as narrative, very moving as tragedy, it illuminates a part of the strange path that the people of North America have travelled as they came to be what they are.[2]

What is implied here in De Voto's remarks is that this kind of interpretive history is very close to the spirit of literature in that it searches for meaning through pattern and image, through the modes of narrative, drama, and poetry, and it reminds us in every word and in every sentence that there is a human voice and a human consciousness in control of the meaning. In this kind of history, the events that compose the pattern, and the landscape which gives rise to the imagery are factual. In pure literature they may or may not be factual: it does not matter there. In one sense, then, imaginatively conceived history is as close to the true spirit of literature as the so-called historical novel or play, which may, at its worst moments, be merely formalized romance cluttered up with factual historical data of no genuine significance.

Needless to say, then, Howard's book inspired me to write *Riel: a Poem for Voices*. It is fair to ask at this point why I wanted to write a poem about Riel if *Strange Empire* itself was such a powerful and imaginative recreation of that period. It was a question which I asked myself repeatedly during the autumn of 1966. *Strange Empire* is imaginative, but it is – as I have indicated – also history. It recreates those times as vividly as any writer will ever be able to. Howard makes the white man feel ashamed, and fills the sensitive reader with a feeling of tragic loss. But because it is history, and because we come to it and accept it as history, it does not really try to make us see its patterns of meaning as universal. Certainly history *does* make us consider the past in the light of the present; some historians are prone to pointing a moral or two, even predicating a recurring pattern of historical events. But they mean these things, one assumes, in a literal sense. If America is Rome reincarnate, then she may re-enact, literally, the fall of Rome, as Senator Fullbright has intimated. But the truths of literature do not operate this way. When they are valid, their truth is archetypal, rooted in the scheme of things, in the unchanging psyche of man – they are in time, and yet out of it – they apply equally to social man and to man private and indivisible.

5

In the final part of this paper I would like to demonstrate the way in which historical poetry and poetic history are transformed into symbolic poetry whose referents happen to have been of historical interest. Howard caught the essence of the Riel tragedy: the clash of cultures. He saw the nature of the conflict between Indian and American, between Metis and would-be Canadian, as a tragic encounter between two fundamentally different peoples. The conflict is centred on the conception which each group has of the land – its meaning for them and the uses which it serves. Seen in this light the events of the period are tragically predictable. Howard, of course, sides with the Indians and Metis, largely because their philosophy of land was mystical, humane, constructive, and socially harmonizing – indeed it was so powerful that it dissolved racial and language barriers in a way that, from our present vantage-point, seems marvellous.

What *I* wanted to add to Howard's own beautiful and moving account was the *poetic* meaning I felt in this story; namely that what might explain the problems in Quebec (or in Biafra, or Vietnam, or in my own personality, which I had been exploring for seven years in my poems) was the meaning which lay below the surface of the Riel story. If I could find the viable and valid symbols in this story, if I could make people feel them in all their complexity, then perhaps some human light would be thrown upon the dilemmas of 1967.

I had, of course, to find these symbols and put them in a vehicle that would allow them to work. I did this over a period of six months – not in any organized way, for poems never come like that. I did not know what the final pattern or meaning was going to be until I wrote the last section. Rather, my method was to read through *Strange Empire*, seizing on events, images, half-ideas, and starting to write, not at the beginning of things, but anywhere that seemed "right" for the moment. I also re-read Stanley's biography, so that I would be aware of the basic history, but I eventually used very little from his book. Early on, I noticed that Howard quoted extensively from original source materials – letters, notes, speeches, documents – and I found much of my imagery latent in these. This led me to the Reference Library in Toronto where I rummaged through the newspaper file in search of similar materials. Here I found Charles Mair's famous and condescending letter about Rupert's Land (he was beaten with brooms by the ladies of Red River for his disparaging remarks), as well as numerous letters to the editor which gave me an authentic "feel" for the Orange point of view (my own Presbyterianism was of some help also in this matter). I was halfway through the poem before I discovered the form it should take: that of a series of voices, whose contrasting views would, I felt, bring the essential conflict to life, and would also point the way to the deeper and more universally human dilemma which underlay the historical tragedy. Whereas Howard focussed widely on the whole American west, I zeroed in on Riel as a symbol of the Metis viewpoint, and Sir John A. MacDonald and his Orange lackies as symbol for the Canadian viewpoint. Through the verse, I was able to invoke the necessary imagery of landscape and Metis life in a way not open to the historian.

The only major problem which developed was – ironically – that I found so much material in the history and documents which fitted my own vision that I had to distort or invent very little to make the poem work. The only examples of such distortion are a hypothetical speech which I put into the mouth of Thomas Scott and a letter supposedly written by a soldier during the first rebellion. In my previous poems I had changed historical fact at will because I wanted the reader to see exactly what I was doing – making poetry out of history, and not writing poeticized history. The amazing fact about the Riel story is that the poetry is already there, built-in, and there are many more poems and plays to be written from this material. Indeed the tragedy of Riel is at once historical and universal, the property of history and the breeding-place of literature. It remained for me to give it my focus and my words, to make it my personal tragedy, one which I hoped Canadians could read alongside the actual story. Even three years after the event, I still marvel at the fact that history and poetry proved to be so intricately connected that it was almost impossible to write a symbolic poem without re-telling the history. Perhaps it is at this very meeting-point that history and poetry get closest to those myths which underlie both of them. And Mr. Lacey's review simply reminded me of what I had known all along.

In conclusion, then, *Riel* is primarily a poem, and as poem it seizes within its imaginative grasp the historical Louis Riel and transmutes him into metaphor; it selects those peripheral elements which were associated with that same historical man and his time – the prairie landscape with the buffalo moving timelessly over it like the cyclic drift of the seasons themselves, and the Indian and Metis people who saw with the simple naivete of the natural mind that man was merely an extension of land and season, of elemental soil and animal blood; and it selects those strange men like Macdonald and Scott who pitted themselves so foolishly and ignominiously against the flow and circularity of Nature herself; it takes these men and these circumstances and welds them into a single metaphor – until Riel is defined by Macdonald and Macdonald is defined by Riel, until they have no valid life except that provided by the movement and shape of the poem in which they now participate. No longer do they belong to history; they are the living metaphors of poetry.

And they speak as metaphor only because they have been transmuted through the imagination of one man living in one time and one place. And they have meaning only if that man has found in the vital elementation of his metaphor a truth which is compatible with his own sense of being, working beneath his own time and place to elucidate that sameness of feeling which adheres in the original historical events. Moreover, this wondrous fusion of the poet's spirit with the spirit of an historical figure like Riel in the symbolic forge of a poem can only convey its meaning to those readers who, coming at it from the outside, can recognize this spirit – calling on their understanding of the history which generated the metaphor, and responding to the poem as verbal construct, so that it stirs in them that elusive mythological dream which sleeps just below consciousness.

And so the elements which once belonged to history become transmogrified through the mind of the poet into a metaphor which becomes the common poetry of all those who can read and respond. Moreover, it is only because we, as humans, can and do respond to history in poetic terms that we can speak with assurance of a Canadian mythology – a mythology which is ours because we, as Canadians, unconsciously share it. And through the consciousness which poetry awakes in us, we are able to bring it to light, and know it.

These are the grand intentions of any poet who dares to call upon history as metaphor. Whether *Riel* achieves them, even partially, must be decided by those who confront it, honestly, as literature.

Notes

Edge, 9 (Summer 1969), p. 130
Ibid, p.131.
Joseph Kinsey Howard, Strange Empire (New York, 1952, p. 17.)

Teaching the Canadian Mythology: A Poet's View

After ten years of writing poems, mainly on Canadian historical subjects, I discovered that, like all serious poets, I had been a maker of myths. This should have come as no surprise to me and yet it did. Perhaps I was just too busy writing the poems to worry about such larger critical and affective aspects of the literature to which I was annually contributing. But events in this country during the past five years have compelled me (and many others) to think more carefully about the significance of our literature in relation to Canada as an emergent "nation".

Myth, of course, is an elusive word, one that has been used, willy-nilly, to bolster the arguments and underpin the hypotheses of critics, psychologists, sociologists, historians, poly-sci enthusiasts, ad-men, and politicians of every blush and hue – each in his own way, perhaps, questing for the golden key to our lost identity. In fact, this quest has become the national pastime, the Canadian quiz-game with myth as the secret word. I have no intention of reviewing or commenting upon the many-splendoured meanings of myth nor the dreary uses to which they have been put. I wish merely to define, as precisely as I can, the way in which myth operates for me as a poet, and mention some of the significant ways in which, I feel, it bears upon the question of our identity, both personal and public.

One "myth" (to use the word in its most common and least fortunate sense) which should be swept aside at the outset is the mistaken notion that we have no identity, or at best a very nebulous one, and therefore, instead of discovering it or bringing it to consciousness, we must somehow *create* one – and fast, before the nasty Americans or the upstart Quebecois overwhelm us with their own clearly delineated cultures. It is this silly notion which has diluted our collective energies and distorted our national goals for the past two decades. To put the record straight, and quite simply, we *have* an identity because we *are* and *have been*. We are and have been occupying this space called Canada for three centuries; for over a hundred years we have referred to ourselves as a nation, and have, more or less, behaved as if we were one. What kind of nation, what sort of people, what forms underlying our national purpose, our common pursuits, our destiny – these are legitimate questions, even yet, one hundred and four years after the official natal rites. However, as I suggested, this country, at least its English-speaking portion (and I suspect, despite the ruder noises, the French-speaking section as well) – seems gripped with an anxiety approaching hysteria and manifesting not a little paranoid-schizophrenia, a blind and self-defeating fear that maybe, after all, we don't exist. Our mirror is a window. Well, it just isn't so. We have existed, and we do.

To argue this point fully would require a separate (and longer) paper, but let me just mention several pertinent points at this stage. Northrop Frye has noted that this kind of anxiety over identity leads to the creation of a social mythology. And much of our identity-hunting in Canada has been of this variety – with all its inherent dangers: self-delusion, commercialization, and ultimate loss of true identity. For our true identity can only be realized, as it has been in each of us as individuals, by questing within, not without, by moving below the surface patterns of our everyday life to that area just beneath consciousness, where the forms of our feeling are known to lie, and where we can apprehend them, free from the pressures and the mirages of the chaos above. This is precisely what the adolescent, what each individual who seeks to be uniquely human, must do. It has its dangers, no doubt, for both individual and group. But one of the dangers is not that we will find nothing. What we will find are the myths, the blueprints which have given and will continue to give our lives, separately or collectively, their unique *curve of meaning*. We may not like what we see, but it exists, and is real enough.

The second point to be made here is that the arts, and literature in particular, have traditionally been the repository for myths, the myths of the individual writer fashioning his work of art and through it the myths of the society out of which and for whom he is writing. (I will elaborate on this further on.) In brief, the mark of a nation, or society, or civilization, as Kenneth Clark reminds us, is its culture, its myriad art-*forms*. Canadians have had a literature, of some kind, from the very beginning. This literature has steadily grown in magnitude and quality; and because it is literature, it does contain myths, which because of their peculiar nature will tell us what we were, where we thought we were going, what we are, and might become.

But how? What is myth in this restricted literary sense? In what way can it provide us with forms of identity? Northrop Frye has dealt extensively (and accurately, I feel) with literary myth in what I would call the critical or general sense. I would like to come at the problem from the inside, from the point of view of the poet who "makes" myths, in order to clarify some crucial points about their nature and the manner in which they operate in literary works.

For the poet, there are three areas of concern ("levels" if you will) in the making of poem: 1) words and rhetorics, 2) symbols, and 3) myths. He begins with words, with what they can express, and what they can be made to do rhetorically. Rhythm and logic and grammar and sound and genre come into play. In a sense, the identity-game begins here. In the quest for words and their rhetorical patterning, the poet is seeking to define in himself what heretofore has been indefinable, or merely vague or shapeless or inchoate. But words, as rudimentary symbols, give back as much meaning as they give off. For the poet this is always a symbiotic process: the self and the language of the self, not identical but *identifying.* Rudimentary word-symbols, grammars, rhetorics – all move easily into the area of literary symbolism. There is no difference here in kind, only of intensity, focus, portability and the potential for interaction. A symbol is a cluster of minor "symbols" (metaphor, character, action, etc.) but more than the sum of its contributors. Consequently, it will say more – will give off more meaning and give back more than the poet expects. At both levels, word and symbol, the aim is to create a *rhetorical brilliance*, in which the penumbra carries the meaning out as well as in. In each instance, the poet is identifying in himself what has been only potential. And, of course, at this point, there are really no clearly marked "levels".

It must be stressed here, too, that this process is exploratory. In the best poems, the true poems, words and symbols have a way of "choosing" themselves. It is more accurate to say that meaning is found or discovered rather than created. Identifying, or knowing one's identity, is an act of discovery, of disclosure. The meaning is there: to be revealed, not promulgated.

I emphasize this point because when the poet moves toward myth the exploratory nature of his work is heightened, becomes infinitely more subtle and "mysterious" (i.e., less easily definable). Myth, in the poem, is the deepest shape of meaning, the point of closest identity between the self and its defining language. It can only be reached (revealed, discovered) through the other two layers or textures of the identifying process. Which is to say that the poet must find his words first, he must make *them* mean so deeply that they take on new configurations and become symbols for him to be re-worked until they too are *brilliant* filigrees of meaning. At this point, if he is lucky enough and good enough, the myths will reveal themselves. For, in one sense, myth was the pattern that was there all along (or seemed so), that was influencing, that was ordering the configurations underlying the rhetoric at both levels. Seen from another angle, it is the pattern created by and yet creating the complex of word and symbol. (Which comes first is a question much debated for centuries and, for the poet at least, not really relevant.)

The general point I'm driving at here is that the poet cannot start with myth. He does not choose it; he works toward it, and finds it. ("Bad" poets and "bad" poetry will probably not conform to the rule, but this is a separate, if not less interesting, problem.) The reader of poems re-enacts the process, beginning with the surface rhetoric and working in and out, back and forth. Thus he is able to identify, through the language of identity, the myth and all its meaning. He is able to recognize a sense of self "other" than his own, and insofar as he is affected by the poem, may identify elements of his own self. If the poet belongs to the reader's own culture, or nation, the common elements of the symbol-patterns (the mythology of the poem) may be more numerous and recognizable than otherwise. Besides the universally human nature of the myths discovered, there will be a level of identification which can only be described as *nation-al*. For what is a nation but a collection of *othernesses*, some of whose elements are mutually felt and understood by its individual members?

Let me illustrate the foregoing by reference to some of my own recent work. I have to date written poems about Dollard, the Jesuits, Hudson, La Salle, Champlain, Riel, and Hearne. These figures, for me, have served the function of symbols. They have been able, through the poems I have built around and out of them, to tell me things about myself. This is the prime motive for writing – the self seeking a language of identification. But I did not choose these personages in any literal sense. I have always read widely and erratically in Canadian history. Certain figures would hold my interest more than others. If this interest seemed inexplicable to me in ordinary terms, I would try writing a poem. There was something to be explained, discovered. Always I began with the poem, the words. I could tell after a few lines or one or two sittings whether or not the words had any *brilliance* to them. If they did not, I abandoned the work. Certain figures, despite several attempts, yielded nothing; e.g., Sir Guy Carleton, an adolescent idol of mine; or Brébeuf, whose place as eventually taken in my "Coureurs de Bois" by a fictional priest who seemed more compatible. Five years later, I was able to write a quite different poem about the great Jesuit ("Brébeuf on the Cross"). What I am saying is that the symbol cannot be chosen consciously, and that the serious and honest poet can determine the integrity of his symbols by testing them operationally at the level of word and rhetoric. They must be revelational not expository. When the words begin to come easily the symbol takes shape through them, and the basic rhetoric of the poem asserts itself; e.g., mode, genre, line-length, rhythm, tone. At some point during this initial stage of writing, the symbols feel "right" and the poem proceeds, with the poet working at both levels simultaneously, making the minor symbol-clusters come together, and glow through the words asserting them. *Riel*, for example, begins to work against the backdrop of prairie, Metis pantheism, Catholic mysticism and the set of counter-symbols represented by Sir John A., the Orange order, Ottawa politics, etc., and the whole design begins to emerge. At this point, the underlying myths may begin to be felt – like shadows, tensions, mirrors within mirrors. Seen from afar, their outline is simple, as Frye suggests: a quest, a tyrannical father over-thrown, the rape of innocence, a prideful fall. To see myth in these general, critical terms is a useful activity, providing the reader with a framework for his reading which is as wide and as deep as the human psyche itself, and a backdrop for those myths which he will encounter "live" within the work of art.

For what I have been trying inadequately to describe above is the poet's discovery of the *myth alive* and the reader's re-discovery of these identifying symbols as he reads. In its living state, the myth is not simple in substance or in outline (though an outline is visible and can be generalized); it is web, and filigree, and labyrinth – where the spaces mean as much as the lines. It is the structure on which all the rest has been built, and yet can only be felt through the flesh it gives shape to. But to call it structure is not wholly accurate, for it has force, and power, a potentiality for movement, for generation. So that the poet, even as he feels his poem close around the myth and reveal it, is aware that the "structure" is but a temporary arresting, the live myth caught and held, for the moment.

Let me illustrate again from my poem *Riel: A Poem for Voices*. As I read the story of Riel in several source books, I knew I had to write a poem about him. Even as I read I could see images coming up at me, could hear words and phrases rehearsing themselves in my head, could even sense the broad outlines of symbolic patterns, a glimpse of the myths lurking below. So the poem began, not at the beginning, but in the middle and moving toward either end. As the words came and the form coalesced (dramatic/narrative, individual voices, long line modulating to short line and first-person lyrics, etc.), and major symbols developed, the poem took its own final shape – which turned out to be quite different from what I had initially envisaged. What I asked myself, on more than one occasion as the poem neared completion, was "How do I know when it is finished?" (I had long ago written Riel's "last" speech), "What force or pattern is governing the selection of materials at this late stage?" Near the beginning of a work, after the initial groping, you feel that you are making some conscious decisions, but as it progresses, you seem to work more blindly and yet less arbitrarily, feeling your way, though the way is not necessarily more difficult. Well, *Riel* ended when the last piece was fitted, and I sensed for the first time what the whole thing was about (characters, incidents, images, words, rhetoric, etc.). I felt those myths which had given my poem shape; that were, in the deepest sense, its meaning. And even now, I have to go back and re-read the poem myself if I wish to feel its original power. You can't seem to carry live myths very far. We have suitcases full of dead ones.

What has the foregoing got to do with Canadian mythology and nationalism? Just this. The myths in genuine literature are honest. They are deep identifying symbols. Our literature, and the mythology it embodies, is thus a repository of "national" symbols. It will help to explain what we are. It will not *create* an identity for us, but will reveal the one we already have.

To be more specific about how this works: each symbol in a poem is at first a *private* one, subsumed by the personality and words of the poet. But it is also public, just as language itself is both personal and social, relative and absolute. The words are the poet's, but they belong to others as well, as they *mean* in ways beyond his control. By the mere act of identifying himself through the medium of language, the poet has made his work and that part of himself involved in it, public property. In this light, the discussion between public and private symbols is irrelevant; they are merely more or less recognizable. The point here is that the works of our poets are public documents to be read so thoroughly that the myths shine through. Secondly, the poet, as person, is one of us, part of this nation, having shared the same environment, the same values, the same history, the same schooling; thus, his person, or self speaking the language of the self, will be *other* than us, but an other more like us than we might suspect or hope. His words, his symbols, his myths will be identifiable and identifying in the only way that humans have of sharing experience and defining themselves as a social group. Our literature is there, and it is important.

The myths which it embodies are significant in at least two ways. First, a wide reading in our literature, set against a background of the best in English literature, will reveal the kinds of myth common to our time and place (past and present); that is to say, that out of the whole range of possible human myths, Canadian writers have chosen these kinds. For example, can we not learn a considerable amount about ourselves by discovering that pastoral myths have always been of prime interest to our poets and novelists? Or that, as Frye and others have noted, there is a distinctly apocalyptic tendency in our best literature? Journeys and quests abound. On the other hand, we don't find many Ulros or neon jungles (not yet). In brief, this kind of criticism, in which myth is generalized for the sake of analysis and comparison, is a valuable way for a nation to begin to discover its "lost" identity.

But the second way is much more significant and valuable, and is the one I am particularly promoting. It involves coming at the *myth alive* and experiencing it both emotively and intellectually. Any analysis of such myths would entail comparing the subtle and elusive differences between this pastoral myth and that one – the pastoral quality or feeling of *Sunshine Sketches* and, say, the peculiar urban-rural tension of Souster's poetry. Or the particular nature of many of our quests which are essentially different from their American counterparts; where the enemy is more likely to be space, the nothingness of north, where the dominant feeling may be a sense of estrangement from the mother-culture, and the illumination at the end no more than an existentialist glow. It is at this level of reading and criticism that literature will yield to us its identifying icons, where the *myth alive* is felt through the individual work, and compared, both instantaneously and in retrospect, with other works of similar scope and power. For here one comes closest to touching the meaning sought after by both poet and reader. Here one catches the unique identity of the individual poet in the very act which makes that identity a public and universal artifact. I may have "chosen" Louis Riel as a private symbol and worked him into a poem in order to discover certain things about myself, but the language I was compelled to work in, indeed the symbols themselves (Riel, Sir John A., the events of 1870-85), belonged from the outset to the people of

Canada. So the poem is at once intensely private and hopelessly public. As a Canadian of a certain type, what I discovered about myself is also what is there for each Canadian to discover, or rediscover, for himself.

Before this starts to sound overly pompous, let me just say that what one finds in the literature may be trivial or important. It depends on the work. But all serious literature will yield information of *some* significance. Let us once and for all set aside the irrelevant arguments about "quality"; let us temper our paranoic inclinations, and seek to eradicate the neo-colonialist sensibility within each of us; in brief, let us get on with the job of taking our literature seriously, of reading it deeply and widely, of developing a genuine critical tradition in which mythology is given its just due. And since criticism, as Frye has noted, is ninety per cent concerned with teaching, let us promote our literature and its mythology throughout the school system. Let us teach it until it speaks for itself.

The country we discover will be our own.

Surviving and (Occasionally) Surfacing

One of the advantages of reviewing a book late in the season – I have read/heard at least a dozen reviews/commentaries on Margaret Atwood's *Survival* – is that much of the ground has already been covered. [It should be noted here that the book is still in print, reprinted with a new introduction in 2004]. One is able to review the book *and* the reviews, coming in somewhere near the middle of the ongoing discussion. For example, it is safe to say that the following consensus has already emerged about Atwood's delightful doomsday book: 1) it is an important contribution to Canadian criticism whether or not one accepts its premises or detailed argumentation; 2) the 'victim' framework is clumsy and heavy-handed, but gradually fades away towards the middle of the book; 3) the chapter on animal imagery is brilliant; 4) each chapter contains more individual critical insights than a volume of our so-called scholarly essays; 5) the teacher's apparatus, while often constraining the flow of argument and somewhat limiting the selection of works to be examined (e.g., availability, contemporaneity), is nevertheless useful food for the under-nourished classrooms of the country; 6) Miss Atwood shows laudable modesty (typically Canadian?) in not referring to her own excellent work to support her thesis, but does show an irritating preference for Anansi authors and a decided lack of decorum in ignoring or slighting old favourites like Callaghan, MacLennan, Davies, et al; 7) there is (dare we believe it?) hope for the future.

In general, I can and will subscribe to this eminently reasonable, composite assessment, partly to save time but more importantly to save space for three somewhat random probes below the glittering surface of *Survival.* For it seems to me that the accolades heaped upon the book are as much a symptom as a sign of the current state of our critical affairs. There is much to be praised (see below), but our approbation should surely be tempered by the knowledge that *Survival* is not only an important 'statement' but is being accepted and promoted as just that: the big critical book of the season, the decade (twenty weeks on the Exeter *Times* best-seller list!). Thus it is safe, and proper, to conclude that its underlying assumptions about the nature of Canadian society and literature are being taken seriously. And given the present state of understanding among the teachers of Canadiana (fervent but ingenuous, the passion of virginity), such seriousness can be dangerous. Without intelligent and in-depth criticism by those who plan to use the book as a 'thematic guide', the results for teaching could be disastrous. We must not allow our sense of awe at the multiple insights in the book (which are considerable and delivered with wit and precision) to overwhelm us so much so that we forget this is a *thesis* book, first and last. It was cunning of Atwood, though not necessarily deliberate, to mesmerize us with her brilliance in those middle chapters so that by a kind of 'proximation' or a particularly leaky form of osmosis, we are lured into a state of acceptance: surely, if chapters two to eleven are bursting with critical power, then the 'conclusions' in chapter twelve must have some validity. And so on.

The critical question, then, is to consider the statements in *Survival* as a whole, parts of a single argument; and this in spite of the author's carefully worded disclaimer in the Preface. One way of doing so, short of writing another book, is to probe here and there below the waters to discover whether the surface reflects the currents underneath, or, where those currents or misty bottom sands are in themselves interesting, whether or not they derive their meaning from the surface moving over them. Here are three such probes.

First, the four basic positions of the victims, which have received much attention already. But have the right questions been asked? For example, although one might agree that the psychological states outlined in the four positions may be readily observed all around us, in what sense can we say that only Position Four is creative? A careful reading of all positions reveals that not only are these states psychological in nature, they are *judged* from a psychological perspective; for example, it is, *a priori*, 'good' to know who the 'real' enemy is and thus free oneself from his (its) power. By implication, then, all those unfortunate victims in Position Two are suffering from delusions when they ascribe their anxiety to Fate; or to the deterministic movement of time and space around them, so vast it cannot be absorbed let alone comprehended; or to the mysterious actions of God or the Anti-Christ; or merely the loneliness of prairie or tundra, the panic of being 'bushed' – all these must be seen as hallucinatory, paranoic transference. At best we can move up to Position Three where we recognize the unreality of such childish fantasies, but fail to do anything about them. With a single slash of the pen Atwood has cut out

God, the Presbyterian (Calvinist/Jansenist) mode of feeling, the significance of land and space and seasons and the impossible dimensions of time which we Canadians *still* must live with every day of our lives. Guilt, Atwood says, must be overcome, for it is, willy nilly, repressive and uncreative.

I think such implications of the book's thesis must be taken seriously before as well as during our reading of the subsequent 'themes'. We must see what is really being said. Positions One to Three are uncreative and 'bad'; thus all characters presented in our fiction, drama, and poetry (though not necessarily their authors) can be analyzed according to their position on the scale of victimization, and as a result we may 'judge' them accordingly; or we may chart the development of our collective psyche through our literature; or place ourselves as individuals on the scale as we measure our response to each work we read. It is not, then, a question of merely disagreeing with the *application* of the victim schema to this poem or that novel; the schema itself is wrong and wrong-headed. It not only slants the 'themes' which Atwood elaborates throughout the book but it grossly distorts the way we see them; it dismisses many authors outright (Davies, Kroetsch, Hood); it implies a hierarchical arrangement among those chosen which is based on shaky psychological grounds, and as chapter twelve indicates on blatant political ones as well. For example, the statement of land-as-monster theme is, to be charitable, one-sided; it ignores the complex symbiotic relationship found in much of our literature, new and old, and eloquently commented upon by critics like Eli Mandel and Dennis Lee. Even the excellent chapter on animals ignores the *fascination* many writers feel for the animal-victim, the quality of *engagement* between writer and symbol, and the resultant ambience and ambivalence which gives such writing much of its power and most of its truth. In fact, Atwood goes most often for the plot, the outline, and not the radiant image or the fully drawn character rooted in setting. Moreover, her refusal to accept guilt as creative/ destructive (a veritable Canadian obsession) leads to the dismissal or distortion of the work of some of our best writers (Richler, Birney, Pratt, Mitchell, and so on).

It should also be noted that a chronological as well as a psychological progression is suggested in the victim schema: earlier writers tend to describe the Canadian psyche in Position One (Grove); later ones move into Positions Two and Three (Callaghan, MacLennan?) and a new breed of contemporary authors moves (along with the country?) into Position Four. But even a cursory reading of three contemporary novels like *The White Dawn*, *The Sparrow's Fall*, and *Night of the White*

Bear, which are dripping with victims, reveals that any statement about our psychic progress is indeed a tentative one. These novels reveal a variety of victim positions, yet all of them to some degree suggest creative possibility in man. The focus is upon the protagonists caught in a complex web of circumstances, and regardless of any 'progression' achieved (some make it, some don't) the reader is impressed by the quality and dynamic of the struggle itself. For Canadians, the creative act is a complex one: constrained, unmitigated, barely possible, and yet committed again and again throughout our short history. The wonder is that anything gets created at all. Whether the constraints, the creative environment, are 'real' or not, or whether one is 'better' than another, is not the central question. As Atwood says, quoting Frye, it is still for us not "Who am I?" but "Where is here?" Perhaps it would be more proper to say that the great Canadian question is not merely one of surviving, but of enduring. To intimate as this book does that our two hundred-year old questions have been fraudulent is impertinent to say the least.

But to be fair let us put down a second probe. In chapter eight, Atwood discusses Pratt's *Brébeuf and His Brethern* and my own *Riel*. In each case ample evidence is adduced for the victim syndrome, the Canadian passion for egregious loserdom. As usual, her eye for the shape, pattern and plot is acute, but she is puzzled by the 'irresoluteness' or ambiguity of the endings, hinting darkly that neither poet was too certain of his psychic ground. But such confusion is to be expected from those who insist on looking at 'plot' only, or the victim-symbol in isolation from the enclothing rhetoric. If *Brébeuf* or *Riel* ends ambiguously it is because the ambiguity was inherent throughout; Atwood apparently does not wish to accept the fact the Brebeuf and Riel could be locked in Position Two, say, and still manage to engage the reader's sympathy or suggest the possibility of freedom and growth, the illusion, if you will, of full humanity. Such is the power of literature, what marks it off from the various 'pseudologies'. No plot summary or symbolic schema can account for this power. *Riel*, as many people have remarked to me, is, in spite of it all, an optimistic poem. So is *Brébeuf.* I cannot help noting that Atwood's own novel *Surfacing* illustrates a similar 'irresoluteness' of endings. The inner logic and rhetorical shaping of the story indicates that the heroine should indeed 'grow fur' or die trying. Such a conclusion would satisfy one of the basic victim-needs in the Canadian character. On the other hand, the novel actually concludes with the heroine's recovery from her mesmerizing, apocalyptic experience 'underwater'; indeed, she resurfaces and swims back to good old Toronto to try again, wetter and wiser (like many other characters in Canadian fiction). While I was personally unsettled by the latter resolution, both endings are prepared for in the novel; indeed the dual ending may be a strength rather than a weakness. Either way it is Canadian, and readily understandable.

Moreover, when we put down our third probe at the last chapter of *Survival*, we see not only the crude distortions the victim schema may produce when applied to individual works (see, for example, the half-reading of Birney's "Bushed", pp. 55-56, which ignores the rhythm and subtle sound effects of the marvellously ambiguous final line) and individual themes (where is the pastoral, and *Leacock*!), but the dangerous conclusions we are apt to reach, political as well as literary. Atwood reviews what she considers to be a proper sampling of current trends, discovering (behold!) that a new breed of writers has at last blasted its way into Position Four by announcing to all generations of Canadians that it was the United States bogey-man all along who was causing us to repress, transfer, and/or sublimate our feelings of victimization – God, Fate, land, space guilt, separation, isolation, horizontal-vertical tensions, the less-than-noble savage, the new bestiary – all these were temporary illusions masking the single, unarticulated (until now, until Anansi) fact that we are and have been exploited all this time by the American Imperialists. And this is, alas, the implicit statement of the whole book. Atwood reinforces such a conclusion when she selects Ray Smith and Dave Godfrey as bell-wether authors only because they articulate openly the dazzling fact that the Yanks are coming! We don't need a Smith or Godfrey to tell us that bad news; Haliburton will serve nicely. What's more, through the sheer power of language, he can still make us like the Clockmaker more than his pathetic victims. He is also capable of rich ironies, holding out to the reader the possibility of a full vision of the Canadian predicament. But Haliburton goes unnoticed in *Survival*. Moreover, Atwood goes on to suggest that perhaps our new breed will try more *consciously* to create myths we can live with, ones which will have important political consequences. What can be said of such a foolish suggestion? As one of our finest poets, Margaret Atwood simply knows better. Myths are disclosed, not promulgated.

And, identity, as Frye notes in *The Bush Garden*, is still a *local* concern, the psychological reality of the place and time we have inherited. Conversely, our sense of *unity*, our need to survive as a country, is national in perspective and political in nature. The former is inner-directed, the latter looks out to the world. Thus it is that our survival as a nation (despite Atwood's fears) must be left to the public side of our nature, the body politic of which we are all a part. Identity, our desire for psychic survival, will continue, as it should, to be faithfully reported to us by our poets, novelists and dramatists. Whether those reports please us is of no concern to the artist.

I can only conclude that Atwood has written two books here, one inside the other, each an extension of one side of its author: the public and the private, the promulgator and the poet. I think I know which one to trust.

Surviving the Fittest: Margaret Atwood and The Sparrow's Fall

1

One of the difficulties in trying to assess Margaret Atwood's *Survival* is that it is so good. And yet so dangerous. Its power, and persuasiveness, derive from its myriad minor insights into certain authors, novels, poems, etc., and in one major semi-flawed critical revelation. Unfortunately the minor insights are exclusively related to the major thesis of the book, and thus their brilliance is often one-sided, dazzling until you turn them one hundred and eighty degrees.

The major critical motif is, of course, the theme of survival and its concomitant image, the victim. This is unquestionably a significant and generative idea, for even though most national literatures are about survival, it is important to see the particular manifestation of that theme as it relates to the writers' (and readers') of our own home ground. Hence the qualifying victim motif, which is elaborated through twelve chapters in a way designed to induce the reader to accept it as the shaping force of this Canadian/universal theme. Herein lies the danger. Atwood selects only those authors and works related to the survival-victim motif, and particularly those whose work reflects a single side of that pattern. For example, little or no mention is made of the following writers: Leacock, Haliburton, Davies, Kroetsch, Child, Livesay, Waddington, and others who have written eloquently about what it's like to survive in this country. In the same vein, Atwood selects carefully within the canon of a given author; e.g., why discuss Fred Bodsworth's *The Last of the Curlews* and not the more powerful *The Sparrow's Fall*? (both about survival and victims); why *Each Man's Son* and not *The Return of the Sphinx*? This kind of judicious selection occurs often enough to make the reader suspicious that Atwood is really writing a thematic study of one facet of the recurring survival motif.

It is difficult to be charitable here because Atwood tries hard to convince us that her view of survival *is* the great Canadian theme. She reinforces this view by setting up an elaborate victim-schema, a framework against which she not only categorizes 'all' Canadian literary works, but also evaluates them in political and psychological terms. I have commented elsewhere in detail[2] about the weakness in this framework, but let me repeat that the injudicious and wrong-headed confusion of critical and psychological principles constitutes a greater literary sin than any biased selection of images or the over-zealous promulgation of one's pet theme. To suggest, as she does, that only recent authors (rinsed in the House of Anansi) recognize the truth of our victim-state (see *Survival*, pp. 241 and ff.) and that past writers, though they may have touched reality for *their* readers, are to be studied at best as a kind of prelude to the current 'breakthrough' period is not only nonsense but propounds a relativistic theory of literature to which I doubt Atwood really subscribes. Indeed, taken to its proper conclusion, such thinking leads the reader to assume that past literature should be studied with a patronizing eye and a complacent smirk, that Leacock and Haliburton and Callaghan and Mitchell and Crawford and Pratt are merely 'quaint' at best, and at their worst, victims of their own illusions. When the authoress puts their books into one of her three victim-categories, she is, despite the shrill disclaimers, placing both the writer and his elderly readers in the same position. In brief, we are asked to judge a book by its positioning on a non-critical, psychological grid – and one which has political ramifications as well. For only current writers seem to have been perspicacious or courageous enough to have seen that the American Imperialists have been our bogey-man all along, and all that stuff about the land, Nature, God, Fate, Necessity, guilt, courage, love, struggle, endurance – all that was just...well, *stuff.*

Here is the crux of the book's own self-contradiction. *Survival* purports to be a manual for criticism-starved school teachers; its avowed purpose is to show reluctant educators that there is a literature 'out there', vital and tough and worthwhile. And yet, despite the excellence of the victim-motif itself, and the minor points made en route, the pseudo-literary framework and breathy exhalations of relevance and progress indicate clearly that the teacher should start his reading in Can-lit at 1960 and do so within the contrived politico-psychological matrix set up in *Survival.* The point is, we can't do both: we cannot respect our literature, past and present, as a *revelatory* agent in our lives and at the same time apply spurious critical machinery to a serious analysis of it. Indeed, if one reads *Survival* closely, one can feel the tension between these polarities, for Atwood is too good at the literary game for her own good. The force of the 'poetry' comes through even her own qualified analysis of it as 'truth'; what she would have us accept merely as themes (i.e., topics which are elaborative content-variations of the original 'victim' statement) shine through here and there throughout the book as genuine myths. And most of these, as critics like Mandel, Mathews and Lee have pointed out[1], are concerned with struggle, with endurance, with the quest for grace in the land God gave to Cain.

One hopes, then, that those teachers who read this book will go for the poetry and not the politics; will sift critical analysis from psychological cant; will be directed into the literature and out to the richer criticism available for those diligent enough to seek it out. In some ways, as I've indicated, Atwood is brilliant, one of the fittest amongst us to tackle an overview of our literature – both her reputation and her ability have marked her off. But this may be a case where we the readers will just have to survive the fittest.

2

But how? Northrop Frye has said that much of criticism takes the form of teaching and so it should.[3] In ideal terms, teaching, whether it be in the schools or universities, is the examination of a literary work by teacher and student in a variety of dynamic situations with a view to seeing the text as both text and context. It presupposes a live and continuous response to the work, in which critical and rhetorical skills can be brought to bear upon it; a variety of personal and individual responses can be elaborated toward consensus; and the cultural context of reader, writer, and work can be applied as required. Teaching is one of the highest and most subtle forms of explaining. It has, for the study of literature, the value of continuous feedback, the dynamics of group-response, and the systematic application of acquired skills. It is under such conditions that the *myth alive*[3] is most likely to reveal itself; not the theme but the shape of the theme which vitalizes the surface elements in a new way, gives to them not only a startling order, but a luminosity of detail which leads one to describe its effect as *revelatory*.

What the teacher needs, then, is information: he needs accurate texts, biographical data, historical and geographical facts, hypotheses, etc.; and then genuinely thematic and/or rhetorical criticism, of the kind which will generate motifs, angles of approach and topics, which the teacher—in the teaching/critical situation—can apply to the specific text under review. We need literary studies like D.G. Jones' *Butterfly on Rock* and Ronald Sutherland's *Second Image*, but we also need first-rate cultural approaches in which the related arts, history, geography, and sociology are used as angles of focus on the literature (just as literature forms a part of these other disciplines). But in the last analysis it is likely to be the teacher and his class working with the text who are going to feel the full revelatory thrust of literature, its genuine myth-making power.

3

Let me now illustrate the foregoing. I have mentioned that Atwood discusses Fred Bodsworth's fine novel *The Last of the Curlews* because she finds the curlew an apt symbol of the victimized Canadian. Certainly there is a haunting pessimism in the book as the bird, the last of its species, struggles to find a mate in order to perpetuate his kind. He loses, of course, faced with storms, cold, fatigue, and the indifference of whatever powers control Nature. Just when he seems to have found a mate and won his battle for survival, the female is shot by an unthinking human. What Atwood zeroes in upon, naturally, is the plot and the cast of characters, and naturally she finds gloom, doom, and death at the hands of outsiders (those nasty Americans again?). Such criticism is at the level of what we may call plot/theme/image analysis. It is where most of us begin. But an elaboration of this level does not reveal the meaning here. Indeed it may obscure the meaning, for there is as yet no analysis of the language, the point of view, the nuance of *feeling*. For example, Bodsworth, in spite of the obvious drawbacks, chose to tell the story mainly from the bird's point of view. We hear his voice in and through the prose. So that we come away not with a sense of outrage only, but with a deep sense of the bird's courage, selflessness, 'humanity', and even beauty, along with his overwhelming desire to endure. There is even some sense of a 'state of grace' in parts, a least kind of pact or compact with the malign forces shaping his destiny. Surely this story is much more than a delineation of the victim-syndrome: it's about character, struggle, and endurance. One remembers the bird's flight, his moments of joy, his simplicity; his failure is forgiven, understood.

If *The Last of the Curlews* is treated from the narrow critical focus of *Survival*, what can we say about the omission of any reference to *The Sparrow's Fall* in a book about victims? Here is a story dripping with victims, and what is more written only half a dozen years ago—thus qualifying for inclusion on two counts. But *The Sparrow's Fall*, though it contains ample victim-situations, does not, as far as Atwood's thesis is concerned, have the proper surface shape (it ends happily); and of course, its deep shape, its myth, is nowhere close to being adaptable to her simplistic schema. Let me, then, illustrate what I believe to be a productive kind of criticism by analysing *The Sparrow's Fall* in some detail, a criticism which subsumes image and theme and motif in the pursuit of a higher truth.

4

Jacob Atook is an outcast who becomes an unwilling hunter of the Atihk (caribou) on the Barren Grounds; the caribou in turn are hunted by wolves, and Atook himself is being trailed and hunted down by an avenging suitor. Who can tell the hunter from the hunted? Jacob Atook is also the victim of certain mental and spiritual struggles raging inside him. The white man's priest came to his tribe and converted Jacob, teaching him that God loves all his creatures equally well and one must therefore have charity for them all. But Jacob's own tribe sees the priest and his religion as a corruptive force from the 'outside' world (a symbol perhaps of European or 'American' values weakening the experience and psychological health of the *native* Canadian?). He is thrown out of the community when he marries Niska who, by the aboriginal rules, was betrothed to Taka the hunter, and also goes as far as having the marriage blessed by the priest. Once on their own, Jacob and Niska become the victims not only of the tribe's judgment but of their own lost values and skills. Jacob has been made soft; he is no hunter like Taka; he has forgotten much; and no one dares to go out onto the Barren Grounds in the winter; better to starve to death. Niska has become pregnant, and Taka is searching for their hidden tent, bent on revenge. Jacob is thus seen in the early part of the novel to be the victim of forces not fully in his control; nor does he understand the source of his dilemma.

The threat of starvation, and the imminent death of his wife and unborn child drive Jacob out onto the perilous Barren Grounds, and for several chapters he enacts the role of bumbling Canadian anti-hero: he loses his way, allows his enemy, Taka, to get onto his trail, loses part of his gun, and is unsuccessful not only in finding a caribou to kill but in shooting anything to keep himself alive. At last he discovers the trail of a single caribou, separated from the herd. Desperately he tracks it down, trying to forget that Taka is close behind him, perhaps only waiting his moment. But when he comes upon the caribou it turns out to be a female about to give birth. Jacob cannot bring himself to kill it; after all, if God sees the sparrow fall, then surely he is watching over this most precarious of births in the winter wilderness. Jacob's 'love' (and deep empathy with a pregnant female) wins out, and he lets it go. Then he sits down to figure out the implications of the priest's theory of the universe. Using pine cones and a simple mathematics, he tries to lay out in the snow the successive generations of caribou as they would look if his people (and the wolves) did not kill them. He gets confused, of course, but dimly begins to realize that there would be far too many caribou for the food available, that somewhere along the chain of life, death is necessary, and good. His faith shaken, he begins the difficult task of remembering the old ways. Perhaps unconsciously (certainly symbolically) he loses his gun in the snow, and when on the brink of starvation fashions a bow and arrow which he uses to shoot the ravens come to feed on his 'carcass'.

Renewed by this grim food, he takes up the trail of the caribou again. When they meet this time, the female is about to give birth in the shelter of a small woods; but despite his new resolve, Jacob still hesitates. This time it seems to be mainly because of his own latent feeling for the distressed and helpless animal. Here is a crucial point in understanding the novel; Bodsworth is suggesting that the source of our victimization is not merely external; Jacob feels for the caribou, and so does the reader. For the author takes time to describe the caribou's life in detail, and the reader as well as Jacob sees that life as an analogue to the Indians' own situation. Jacob's victimization at the hands of the priest and his own tribe is subsumed by larger considerations: the exigencies of this vast space, this vicious cold, the limited supply of food—these necessities create victims of the caribou and his desperate hunter alike, and without discrimination. Even the wolves are seen not as predators (analogous, say, to the outside oppressors) but sympathetically. Again, ample space is given to describing them: they have a hard life, too; they are victims of supply and demand in the precarious food-chain. Bodsworth casts each victim-group in a noble (not romantic) framework. The caribou endure, the female sacrifices herself for the young; the wolves cull the old and the sick, obey their own inner laws; Jacob Atook, who now thinks he fully understands his original role, does kill the caribou, uses native cunning to undo Taka and prove himself a hunter and a man; and, all the while, beginning to clarify the source of his original failure: the influence of the priest's ideas.

What is important at this point in the novel is to feel the full range of implication in the victim-symbol. All victims (and the animals are characters as much as the humans) are viewed as subject to the weather: the cruel winter, the blinding snow (Jacob has to re-remember how to make sunglasses out of sticks), the ceaseless wind. Bodsworth details the manner in which each victim copes, survives, and endures according to his kind. It is in their endurance that they gain our sympathy, in the quality of their response to necessity, animal or man. Thus the *source* of victimization at any one point in the story is diffused and complex. Even without the priest's unhappy sparrow-theory, an Indian's life is hard enough. He is a victim of his place, his time, of forces beyond his own understanding or that of the all-seeing priest. Jacob's proper response is to survive, to endure, and because he is a man, not an instinctive beast, he must think and feel, work out his own salvation within the partially visible framework of the incomprehensible world he was born into.

Thus it is that when Jacob Atook returns step by step to his original ways and values he becomes the hunter who redeems himself, foils his human enemy, and returns home with the life-saving caribou. But Jacob is human; and his world for better or worse is now touched irrevocably by the white man. The Barren Grounds have provided him with a temporary setting (practically and symbolically) for his rite of passage. Now he's going home; and home is not the same necessity as this winter proving ground.

So we have the novel's final brilliant turn. Jacob's own ineffectualness has cost him many days of wasted effort; if he has returned to belief in the natural laws once more, Jacob knows that by even the most optimistic calculations his wife should be dead. The fact that he even dares to hope indicates that his conversion to aboriginal ways of thinking has not been complete. He arrives back home to find his wife not only alive but well. She had managed to catch a fish through the ice, a feat which Jacob must consider beyond any reasonable probability. Niska caught only one fish, but it was "a big one" she informs him. For a moment he thinks it must have been the work of that same magic that had brought him first wind of the caribou. It must have been *Manito* (the Indian god) and not *Manitou* (the priest's God). Jacob tells her triumphantly, "He doesn't love the sparrow, or the atihk, or anything else." But Niska counters with these questions: "Who brought the *Kahkaki* [wind] when you needed it? Who turned the atihk back? Who brought the snow so that Taka isn't trailing you now?" And as Jacob, with much trepidation, feels his child miraculously alive in Niska's womb, she says simply, "And who kept *it* alive, Jacob, when you were sure it was dead?"

And suddenly the reader is as uncertain as Atook himself. The novel concludes with a moment of partial but visionary insight:

For death at the hunt's end did not destroy, it was only an exchange of fleeting flesh amid life's permanency...this death and living, but without contradiction or negation, a warp and woof of the same inseparable cloth. For that was the thing the gods had made. (p. 255)

The reader is left with the feeling that although all characters (animal and human) are victims when viewed as individuals, when seen as part of the vaster scheme of things they give fresh meaning to the word 'victim' itself. It is not enough (as Atwood would have us do) to find the efficient cause, place the blame outside or in, sublimate or fantasize; one must *feel* the role of victim in relation to the other victims one interacts with; and each must play his role rightly, must first of all survive, then learn to endure, while at the same time thinking and feeling one's way toward a proper place in the scheme of things. It implies also an understanding of what *can* be known and what is ultimately beyond knowing. Jacob Atook has survived and become respected in his own eyes (and the reader's) precisely because he has worked out a proper set of *human* values in the cauldron of brutalizing experience. He does not merely slough off the 'corruptive' value-system of the outsider, nor does he make himself purely aboriginal again (Bodsworth, being Canadian, seems instinctively to reject the noble savage myth, the Rousseauesque retreat to the territory'). In fact

Atook is greater in our eyes than Taka, the 'uncorrupted' savage who follows the old ways, because he (Jacob) has been able to absorb part of the priest's value-system, has integrated it with his own personality and necessities, and emerged infinitely stronger and more completely human. And by compelling the reader to identify with all the victims and by having us empathize with Jacob's own ambivalent sympathies, his emerging thought, his basic good conscience, Bodsworth presents us with what we can only call a *creative victim*. In fact, what Niska is asking him at the end is: 'Is it not possible that God sent the priest to us for a purpose?' The answer to that naive Christian question is embedded deep in the fabric of the whole novel.

In one sense, then, *The Sparrow's Fall* is a brilliantly elaborated allegory of part of the complex Canadian experience. Paradoxically, though, its power derives from its *not* being explicitly allegorical; not even symbolic. Bodsworth, the naturalist, weaves together the complex interrelationship of man, beast and landscape by describing them in intrinsic detail, and by setting their actions side by side without comment. This method seems a characteristically Canadian one: the animals are victims, but not merely the hunted; moreover, they are not described solely from the perspective of their interaction with the hunters; they have a life of their own not as mere symbols or analogues, but as characters. So that not even the casual reader may view the novel in narrow allegorical or psychological terms. Bodsworth's methods give to the concept of creative victim a depth and resonance which compel us to move beyond the plot structure, the symbolic outline, the easy categorization of our most complex human dilemmas.

The Last of the Curlews truncated by a spurious criticism, and *The Sparrow's Fall* not mentioned at all—what credence can we give, then, to Atwood's thesis? I think we can accept the victim-motif as a significant idea to be explored in the coming years with the best of our traditional critical methods. In the meantime, scepticism may, understandably, run high about accepting our victim-role in the confined psycho-politico terms outlined in *Survival*. For, though suffering be the badge of all our tribe, it need not lead us to collective paranoia. Suffering, guilt, the anxieties of time and place are conditions every Canadian knows first-hand. Surely literature, seen aright, can liberate us long enough to permit an occasional glimpse of ourselves as we really are.

Notes

For a detailed analysis of this lop-sided syndrome in *Survival*, see Robin Mathews. "Struggle and Survival in Canadian Literature," *This Magazine is About Schools*, VI,4 (Winter 1972-73), pp. 109-124.
See Eli Mandel, "The Study of Canadian Culture," *The English Quarterly*, IV, 3 (Fall 1971), pp. 15 24. Robin Mathews, "Canadian Literature: the necessary revolution," *English Exchange,* XV, 1 (Autumn 1972), pp.2-13. Dennis Lee, "Rejoinder," *Saturday Night*, LXXXVII, 9 (September 1972), pp. 32-33.
Northrop Frye, *The Educated Imagination* (Toronto 1963), p. 55

Reference

Fred Bodsworth, *The Sparrow's Fall.* Toronto: Doubleday, 1967.

History as Public and Private Metaphor: The Question of Intention

The Uses of Metaphor

Much as the sense of place does, the figures and events of our historical past become part of our psychological ground. Our parents, our relatives and neighbours, the imagined creatures we all people our childhood with – these, along with the stories and legends that surround them, become psychological elements and categories by which we absorb and find meaning in the more distant figures and events of our country's history. In a sense one can only know as much about one's country as one knows about one's self. And since local and regional history, particularly of the narrative/anecdotal kind, reinforced by the immediate presence of the regional geography – since it will be learned in close communion with the child's personal history/geography (his home ground) – the imposition of the wider history of the nation will always be secondary. This is always true, at least in psychological terms. Canadians, as Frye has noted, are regional, then national.

Nevertheless, the correspondences and analogies of literature and the arts in general, the imaginative habit if you like of associating the known with the alien, the possessed with the fear of 'otherness', allows the child to move easily from the 'vast plain' of his backyard to the 'Indian country' of his uncle's farm and later on to the prairie of Riel or Big Bear. And if the imaginative habit has been nurtured well (that is, not interfered with by the schools or other over-zealous institutions), it will not matter whether the man is on a camping trip to Batoche or reading *The Temptations of Big Bear* – the feeling generated by the correspondence set up between the primary psychological symbol (the child's backyard) and the progressive secondary ones (regional spaces, actual prairies, verbally rendered ones, etc.) will be equally powerful in their own right. Similarly, the cowboys and Indians we all role-played, the fabulous tall tale of great-uncle's pioneer days, the wicked goings-on of the nearest 'big city', the death of great-grandma at two hundred years – these primary experiential symbols will, if encouraged, seek their own wider correspondences in the world of actual event, recorded histories, and imagined ones.

In each case, of course, the kind of meaning will and should differ: most of us try to create a life for ourselves based on some definition of what really happens to us. But we also depend on our memory to interpret what we've recorded as past reality, though we ought to be aware of what happens in the process (the historiographer's role?). Still others, if encouraged, may find a special use for those correspondences found mainly in literature; i.e., imagined in somebody else's 'reality'. And sometimes, and especially in present-day Canada, the literature is not only about the poet's history (remembered and invented) but about the recorded and generally accepted version of the nation's story.

How then do we receive and use this latter kind of literature? Often we have been trained to read its poetry as the subjective presentation of another creature like us, and find therein psychological affinities with another human's personal experience (however defined). The poet's metaphors collide nicely with our own: Cohen's lover in *The Spice-Box of Earth* strikes us with the perception we have of ourselves as lovers. What is foreign or unassimilable is ignored or rejected. That's the way much poetry works on us. But if the person is someone we 'know', like Louis Riel or Father Brébeuf or Norman Bethune, how do we accommodate the historical personage as generally received and as privately interpreted through the unconventional historiography of the poet? In brief, how do we approach, understand and use historical poetry?

Incidental and Constituent Metaphor

The problem is not one in reading methodology, but rather a question of intention – the poet's and the poem's. In narrative or novelized history the intention of the text can often be derived by checking the number and kinds of distortions of the accepted facts; by noting through the cumulative detail just how wide an historical canvas is being sketched; by measuring the bias of the author through his tone, voicing, and the process of selection and focus; and, if we're lucky, through the convenience of a preface. But poetry (and this could well include the more poetic forms of fiction and drama: Wiebe's *Big Bear*, Mair's *Tecumseh*, etc.) operate not only within these conventional formats and constraints but also and fundamentally through metaphor, through image and symbol where the questions of intention is more complex. Hence the interpretive issue in historical poems may best be discussed in the light of how metaphor itself operates in poetry. For our purposes we shall isolate two basic kinds of metaphor and then examine their intentional implications for historical poetry.

Most poems, historical or otherwise, contain *Incidental Metaphors*; that is, comparisons which meet an immediate need in a particular poem or part of a poem. They are used to extend our knowledge of the objects, individually or collectively. They are *outer-directed*, taking us always away from their own structure as word-symbols and out toward the object, persona, action or thought of the poem, so that we find no need to return to them as tropes or to examine the ground out of which they sprung. Incidental metaphors are vehicles – invisible when used well – directed out to larger and more visible poetic purposes. Collectively they may form sustained sequences of comparison – what are often called image patterns or sustained metaphors – which yield larger and more systematic meaning. Here is an example from a non-historical poem (one of my own):

Skating Out

What are these
miniatures moving out of the
encoving dark, the
marvellously one- mooned sky oh
open utterly, they
slide seaward on the
sudden ice/earth but
there is no sea-
sound, no border
line they glide
toward these wing-
less filigrees
rise wide and

loose oh into the
unutterable moon-
curved dark, the
edge of all ice and
no sound but the

bladed silence
ringing starward
                                        these
child-creatures loom
high and wide and
don't they know
there's no horizon
no words when
moons bloom in the
eyes widen their
breath ballooning
they sail the
unuttering oceans of
air
   those
miniatures I last
glimpsed skating
the moon's face

Incidental metaphors abound: children are "miniatures", the dark is a "cove", skaters "glide" and are "filigrees", silence is "bladed", oceans have the sentience to be "unuttering". Such garden-variety metaphors are read (1) initially for their *immediate* meaning in terms of feeling, movement, colour; and (2) for their *analogical* import (how are children "miniatures"? that blooming moon is not only expanding but is, by implication, animate and thus its "face" is anticipated, etc.); here the focus moves always from the tenor (moon) to the vehicle[4] (face) and back to the reconstituted tenor (the moon with a face, etc.); and (3) for any cumulating and recurrent patterns of metaphor (vehicles); e.g., the sea-imagery here ("encoving", "slide seaward", "sea-sound", "sail", "oceans of air"); the idea of borders, edges, horizons; and others. Collectively, then, these *Incidental Metaphors* may raise further implications regarding space, terror and ecstasy. The title may invite yet another reading, so that the incidental metaphors might be regrouped as they relate to aspects of 'skating': are these really children? really skaters? what larger inferences can be drawn from these questions? Most of our best poetry leads us in such directions. Its intention is manifest in the way in which the metaphors are presented and read, and the business of teaching young people to read poetry should be largely taken up with these intentional concerns.

Now the historical poem (play, novel) may well be, in metaphorical terms, of the *Incidental* kind where the author uses comparisons to characterize more vividly a Louis Riel or Big Bear, where the imagery of landscape is rich and detailed and connotative so that the reader's sense of time and place will be exact. And as long as the focus is kept on the personage, action, setting *per se*, one may assume that the intention of both metaphor and literal detail is to present historical action as if it were to be received as *having happened.* Pratt's *Brébeuf and His Brethren*, Coulter's *The Trial of Louis Riel*, Wiebe's *The Temptations of Big Bear*, even Birney's fantasy "The Damnation of Vancouver" are generally of this order and intention. But my own *Riel: a Poem for Voices* only partly belongs here, and raises further questions.

The other part of *Riel* addresses itself to the presentation of *Constituent Metaphor*, a structure that demands a different kind of reading. When the reader has been drawn through the collective incidental metaphors and back to the whole tenor of the poem, and then is drawn back yet again toward the vehicles of the metaphors, so that his interest is focussed on the *ground* from which the metaphors have been struck, and is directed towards the shape or substance or structure of that ground – then deeper and more private and psychological intention may be inferred. For example, in "Skating Out" it is possible that the reader might begin to dwell on the metaphors grounded in sea, ice, space and horizon, which are the source of the individual vehicles earlier described. If so, then the poem's meaning expands even further. But how do we know whether to proceed this far? Is the idea of space and order itself a further, a constituent, metaphor embedded *totally* in the structure of the whole poem? One tests the intention here only by continuing analysis which should yield successively interesting and mutually interdependent layers of meaning. For example, if a reader were to examine four or five poems related to "Skating Out" which contained metaphors grounded in ice, hockey, winter landscapes, etc., he might well be drawn toward an exploration of a common *Constituent Metaphor.* Such recurrences, if they yield satisfactory meaning-patterns, suggest that the poetry's intention is indeed *inner-directed*, drawing us towards the metaphorical ground of the poem itself (voicing, language, symbol structure) and away from (but never completely) the objects *per se* and their literal/connotative presentation. Both aspects are mutually enriched, it must be emphasized, for we may return to the surface only by reorganizing it, for at least a third time, in light of the Constituent Metaphor. But poetry that invites us to read its metaphors constituently is going to prove more difficult to pin down to time and place. History itself may well be the ground for metaphor and not the reverse.

The reader of historical poetry, then, will have to make certain he can distinguish the intention of the poem in regard to its metaphoric presentation. But before examining *how* such distinctions can help him read it successfully, we need to examine intention from its other side: what does the poet himself intend? How is *he* using history?

Private and Public Metaphor

As I've written elsewhere, the poet may well look to historical figures, events and landscapes more or less as a source of Incidental Metaphor for a poetry which is quite subjective in format and intention. Equally he may find a major historical figure and/or set of events which provide the ground for Constituent Metaphor whose intent may be to elucidate the private feelings of the writer: not directed towards the historical figure but towards the poet or his persona, not towards an interpretation of the past so much as a rendering of the present through the symbols of the past. In either case – the private use of history through Incidental Metaphor or the private use of history through Constituent Metaphor (cf. John Newlove's "Samuel Hearne in Wintertime" with Al Purdy's *In Search of Owen Roblin*) – the reader will determine the poet's intention in the following ways: he will, in the first instance, decide whether Incidental Metaphors direct the meaning towards the poet's *present state* and concerns (in Purdy's poem the meaning is as much about the poet as about Owen Roblin and the history of Prince Edward County) or towards the historical figures and actions *per se* (e.g., Pratt's *Brébeuf* or *Titanic*); and second he will determine whether the encompassing Constituent Metaphor, if there is one, creates a personage and set of actions which seem more an alter ego and life for the poet and *his* times, or whether it draws us towards a more mysterious, time-spanning symbol which may cause us to re-evaluate both our common past and our individual present. Poems like *Owen Roblin* and Margaret Atwood's *The Journals of Susanna Moodie* work both ways. There is enough detail and Incidental Metaphor in the latter, for example, to recreate Mrs. Moodie and her life and times over several decades; but the poem is also subjective in intention, reminding us very much of other Atwoodian personae and the poet's customary metaphoric ground (animals, dislocation of space and time, disjunctive narrative, interiorized psychological landscapes), and suggesting, especially through the poem's ending in present-day Toronto, the working out of Constituent Metaphors of existential journeys and quests.

It is important to realize that the poet may use either metaphoric method to compose poems that use history as *Private Metaphor* (i.e., to explain oneself) and as *Public Metaphor* (to explain oneself and the history in mutually significant terms). My *Riel* differs from, say *Brébeuf*, in that it uses Constituent Metaphor for principally private purposes, while *Brébeuf* uses Incidental Metaphor for the public purposes. *Riel* emanated from metaphors the poet found psychologically necessary: he begins with Louis Riel, takes him as psychological correspondent/correlative and then moves in from there through cumulative Constituent Metaphors (prairie-city, rivers-railways, squares-circles) so that the poem means both more and less than mere historical interpretation. On the other hand, *Brébeuf*, through historical detailing and brilliant Incidental Metaphors, recreates for public reading an account of the Saint's life which renders and interprets at the same time. And certainly the intention, both metaphoric and personal, is not to direct us towards the poet and his times nor in towards the symbol structure of the poem, but out to the grand scale of history itself embodied in man's best words.

Though few historical poems are clear-cut in terms of these categories, it is important to apply them if the reader is to know how to accommodate such knowledge as they may provide.

The Reader's Rights

What are the reader's duties beyond determining some of the intentions of poet and poem? What are his rights in the rhetorical contract? In *Riel*, for example, though its intention is towards the private use of Constituent Metaphor, the reader knows, or may easily inform himself of, the public figures and recorded events that provide for its metaphoric ground.[5] In this sense the poem, despite its author's intention, may be regarded as Public Metaphor. Naturally the reader is invited not only to be engaged by the poem as a poem but to set the poet's account of history against the known events and their interpretation by historians. Such comparison merely adds a further dimension to a poem's meaning: the reader may possess the poem's private, self-contained vision and use it as he wishes, and he may also see in its distortions a new range of meaning, one to draw past and present into momentary coexistence. The fallacy he must avoid, however, is trying to read beyond the poem's intentions by colouring them *a priori* with the public facts. He must remember too that in this instance the tension between the poet's Riel and the accepted historical versions is one between history and a private metaphoric rendering of it, and not between two *versions* of the same set of historical events. Literature of this kind is not a version of history but a use of it: the wrong set of questions in these circumstances could set back interdisciplinary Canadian Studies several decades (e.g., Which version is 'truer', poem or biography? Poetry gives the emotional side, history the rational, eh?). On the other hand, with an historical poem like *Brébeuf*, with its more literally directed metaphors and its movement towards an imaginative public statement, the reader may well enjoy the poem as a self-contained rendering of events with incidental metaphoric implications, and then, if he wishes, read it as a version of history to be set against the known and the accepted – albeit a version without the constraints and sanctions of historiography.

History, Metaphor and National Identity

There remains one further intentional problem, especially significant as it relates to the cultural uses of history and literature. Unfortunately the cultural efficacy of historical poetry (literature) is diminished by the fact that Canada is a country whose history, in terms of character and event, is not widely known. Yet, paradoxically, its *places* – its regions, both in past and present tense – are deeply known and intuitively understood by at least a large minority of those who read. Therein, perhaps, lies the explanation for the inordinate amount of description in our novels and stories: we know our secret places and wish to render them in detail for the outsider while proving to the insider that we belong. In a similar vein, our poetry has supported a narrative tradition in the face of insuperable odds: perhaps because we have a need to render the characters and minute events of our past, to tell our story in the old, simple sense, and tune its meaning to the exact rhythms of poetry. Thus it is that poems like *Riel*, *Towards the Last Spike*, *Susanna Moodie*, and more recently Peter Stevens' long work on Norman Bethune are comfortably read as private and/or public metaphor.

But what happens when we go beyond the short-list of the known, the mutually shared and understood? As critic David Cavanagh has pointed out, such communally perceived symbolic figures as Riel and Brébeuf are few in Canada. It is more common for poets to take the partially known or regionally popular figures and literally remake them for the general reader; e.g., Newlove's "The Pride", Bowering's "Hamatra", MacEwan's "Franklin", Birney's "George Vancouver and Skuh-wath-kwuh-tlah-kyutl", and Lampman's "Dollard". Here the poet may begin with the correspondence between the self and the figure he half receives and half makes, and then moves out to the creation of a genuine symbolic historical figure, a Public Metaphor. On one level the poet hopes to tempt the reader into returning to the very history being used as grounds for metaphor in order to have him understand its significance as common heritage as well as its use as a framework against which the poem's private distortions can be measured in further pursuit of meaning. In brief, if the figure is not known, the poet can use him quite comfortably as a private metaphor for a private (subjective) poem, almost as if he had totally imagined him.

But if he wishes to go further, then his reader must sense the intention and read far enough in, and perhaps even around, the historical material. An error in grasping the poem's intention could result in a truncated interpretation. For example, note this excerpt from David Cavanagh's response to *Coppermine: the Quest For North*:

At a time when Canadian writers are scrambling for a mythological basis for their work, one might expect Gutteridge to attempt to raise Samuel Hearne to the level of symbol or archetype of something rooted deeply in whatever it is we call a Canadian consciousness. But it is becoming clear that one cannot raise to the level of mythology historical figures who are not already alive in readers' minds and emotions... The Americans have The Texas Rangers, Al Capone, and more recently, perhaps, the hamburger, but Canada is short on historical archetypes. Louis Riel could be such a figure, and Gutteridge makes good use of him in his poem about the righteous revolutionary cum murderer... It may be that Canada's historical figures have never made it into the emotional reservoirs of Canadians. It may be that our archetypes must be created – fictitious figures based upon emotional truths, such as Rachel Cameron or Hagar Shipley, who are now entrenched as types of two particular kinds of Canadian women.

Hagar and Rachel are important literary creations, but they are not historical and present no related problems of intentionality. Hence the critical error here is not one of interpretation of the poem's structure but of its intention. Cavanagh senses that, unlike Riel, Hearne is not widely known. Therefore he concludes that the poem must be either a successful private/psychological one or else a faulty attempt to raise a culturally significant symbol, such as Riel might be. In fact the poem is both: its principal intention is *private* and its metaphors *constituent*, and once this focus has been recognized, then the public and incidental aspects may be safely responded to. Indeed the original concept included inter-facing pages from Hearne's own *Journal*, but this proved to be too intentionally heavy-handed and was thus abandoned. Nevertheless it demonstrates the urgency one felt to provide *some* common ground against which the private symbols would resonate. In these cases reader and writer may just have to collaborate: surely the result would be wider, more public meanings, not confused ones – provided the question is understood in intentional terms.

Similarly, in a more recent work, *Borderlands*, I have tried in part to recreate from minor historical figures like John Jewitt and the Nootka Indian, Maquina, public symbols that may help to people the empty spaces of our historical consciousness. And of course the land, the landscape, the region *is* there, is real to us, and always provides the esthetic distancing and stability for the more frantic and inescapable subjectivities of the poet's private Necessity.

A Caution

Whether a poem be Public or Private, Metaphorically Incidental or Constituent, neither the poet nor the reader can wholly invent a past nor cause Canadians to know the figures and events beforehand. We work with what we have – precious few common heroes and a deeply felt sense of place, along with a lot of regional and lesser known figures and stories, and side by side with a newly-found will on the part of both reader and writer to make the most of our scarce resources. Knowing what is real about our past and what is true in our literature – and that includes some knowledge of the process of writing itself, its intentions and effects – is all we need for the time being.

Regions of the Heart: The Politics of Literature in Canada

To attempt an essay on regionalism in Canadian Literature at the beginning of the 1980's is not only a critical act but a political one as well. As our politicians have been reminding us, with occasional eloquence, we are a nation with a divided psyche: at once federal and provincial, national and regional, representative and particular. While this may be a universal state of human affairs, for Canadians at this point in their history the tug-of-war between opposing loyalties is immediate, politically crucial, and bewildering. Against all our deepest instincts as a people – however shallowly rooted in this time and place – we feel as if we are being compelled to make a choice, once and for all time. Not that we will – or ever can, mind you – but the very *thought* of being manoeuvred into a position where we have to decide, fills us with the dread of uncertainties, divided houses, lingering doubt and that tenacious, Jansenist guilt so ingrained in the Canadian character. The "Feds," as they are now called, belittle those among us who cleave to the regionalist hope as old-fashioned, as children clinging to the mother-teat. "Come with us," they soothe in another key, "Leave the womb; enter the big, wide world with us." Those who in their childishness demur are branded crypto-separatists – *enfants terribles* brooding on the past till they go mad and what-is-more make the enlightened souls around them uncomfortable.

For the writers of Canada, whatever their views as citizens, the decision has already been taken: with the first line of the first poem, with the initial bloom of a character in the uncharted dark of the imagination. Our writers, like artists everywhere, are separatists at heart, delvers in the soil of their regions. Whatever they turn up we must eventually learn to live with, willy nilly, if we wish to view ourselves as a human community. Their work should not be co-opted, however noble or urgent our motives might be. None of our poets, playwrights or novelists is, in the strictest sense, a nationalist, their own pamphleteering notwithstanding. Which is not to deny that the best and truest of their works may assist us in shaping the community of our dreams, for what the poem forges – out of time, place and the currency of a shared language – is a statement of our being – of our having been and about to become – as real as the War of 1812, the October Crisis or the resurrection of Pierre Trudeau. Because it is regional in its purest form, the poem may, given the chance, inform in a material way that very collective consciousness that helps define the precarious, ephemeral state we call nationhood. To deny the essential regionality of literature is to relegate its role to the peripheral and decorative at best, and at worst to corrupt it utterly in the sleazy service of the State, whose norms, be they benign or malignant, are set by the ruling faction of the moment. Canada does not lack an identity because its writers have not matured enough (not stewed long enough in the national juice) to confect themes of transcontinental scope, but rather because until recently its citizens have not been encouraged to look at the signal, defining, illuminating works of literature surrounding them – poems, plays, novels and stories hammered out of the stubborn carbon of the regions we have staked out for our own.

What is meant by the regionality of literature in Canada? Much has been written on the subject, but mostly (and quite properly) from the perspective of the traditional concerns of literary criticism: the nature of the creative process (the writer in his landscape), the literary history (Confederation poets, West Coast radicals), genres and forms (realism in Prairie fiction, the regional idyll), and psychological/thematic frameworks (Moss's geophysical imagination, Ricou's vertical man/horizontal world, New's articulating West). All of these have enriched our understanding of the regional dimensions of our literature. However, in light of the political implications – that is, the uses to which our literature is put – I would like to re-examine the concept of regionality with a focus not only on the features of the works themselves but on the way in which the community of readers has responded to them. While some attention will be paid to the literary aspects of the works and their effects (immediate and long-term), questions of intention, intrinsic quality and creative process will be dealt with only as they relate to *the context of community response.* Examples will be given from fiction, drama and poetry to illustrate the categories delineated and the community's role in shaping them. No attempt can be made to do justice to all of the appropriate or deserving works that could be mentioned.

What is at stake here is more than just another attempt to define regionalism. A national crisis and a new generation of educated readers are taking our literature where it belongs – into the mainstream of personal and political consciousness. Its entry into this arena, however, has not always been a happy or enlightening one. The internationalists among us (now a beleaguered band) still hurl their charge of "second-rate" against much of the literary canon; the anti-internationalists (self-styled nationalists) are still apt to damn with loud praise every native flower however forlorn (not much but our own); the new breed of nationalists (the federalists) decries the regional bias as parochial (quality notwithstanding), disunifying, and hence subversive; and the regional rump-parties have discovered, somewhat belatedly, the propaganda value of the provincial poem. At the centre of this confusion is not just the conflicting wills and plots of special-interest groups but a fundamental misunderstanding of the nature of all regionally inspired literature and the way in which it operates upon a community of genuine readers.

First of all, regionality encompasses not one but at least three distinct types of literature: the literature of Local Colour, of Spiritus Loci, and of Virtual Place. While these may initially appear to be similar – in content, form and theme – when examined from the perspective of how and why they are received and used by genuine readers (as opposed to exploiters) across a period of time, they emerge as discrete categories, each of which plays a significant but different role in helping us develop a sense of community.

The literature of Local Colour is by definition parochial. It is inspired by and sets out to describe a locality: through the imagery of verse, the characters and stories of fiction, the dialect and social themes of drama. It is grounded in place and fixed in time. To whatever degree it may be fictionalized, its readers, contemporary or future, recognize the place and time, respond to its regional detail, and learn what it must have "been like" there and then. The original appeal of such works may extend only to the readers of that region, or, where particular conditions of the period (promotional activity, publishing policies, topicality, etc.) permit, across the other regions of the country. Beyond the first generation of readers, they may survive locally, as curios, but are largely forgotten by the general community thereafter. Examples of this type are Goldsmith's "The Rising Village", MacCullough's *The Stepsure Letters*, Barr's *The Measure of the Rule*, Scott's Indian verse, Duncan's *The Imperialist*, Stead's *Grain*, Dewdney's *Wind Without Rain*, Baird's *Waste Heritage* and Garner's *Cabbagetown*. I mention these rather than more ephemeral titles like Connor's *The Foreigner: A Tale of Saskatchewan* or Trueman's *My Life as a Rose-Breasted Grosbeak* because the former represent works that have been reclaimed much later by both the regional and general community.

While these, and perhaps others like them still awaiting reclamation, were initially works of Local Colour, fixed in time and place, they have been seen as valuable enough, in some way, to deserve appropriation by a wider community generations beyond their first appearance. They have been elevated by consent into the general canon. (I am deliberately excluding titles revivified solely by and for literary scholars.) Nor is this phenomenon governed necessarily by questions of quality or intention. These writers, like their counterparts everywhere, wrote not for their region but out of it, willing their offspring to the widest readership possible. Surely we have appropriated *Grain* or *Cabbagetown* not because we believe them to be neglected masterpieces but because as citizens of a community of regions set in historical time we want to know more about the places, events and figures of our past: we feel a need to recapture the *specifics* of locales we somehow sense at this moment are important to us. So we return to these works and redeem them precisely because of the Local Colour that initially informed them: the sights, sounds, smells, tastes, wishes and hopes of a past for which we feel a special kinship. Such appropriation tells us more about ourselves than it does about the value of a novel or poem in purely literary terms (whatever they are). Even now the production of Local Colour proceeds apace: Morley Torgov's *A Good Place to Come From* (Sault Ste. Marie) or David Williamson's *The Bad Life* (in Winnipeg during the 1950's) are waiting for some future, caring generation to confer its blessing on them, to bestow on them the epithet "valued". To label works of Local Colour "second-rate", to overpraise their literary quality for spurious political gain, or to slough them off as "merely regional" is both foolish and dangerous. All of them aspired to the essential condition of art – to be cherished beyond their own time and for the values which originally informed them. Only time therefore can be their arbiter. To their credit the last three generations of Canadians have begun to make their own judgements about the literature of Local Colour. In doing so they have thrown into doubt the notion that somehow all worthwhile literature must make itself "universally" comprehensible and valued at the instant of its creation (under the constraints of "universal" standards, of course). Fortunately for Hardy, Faulkner and Patrick White, such silliness has never been taken seriously by mature, confident societies.

The second type of regional literature, that of Spiritus Loci or the Spirit of Place, shares many of the surface features of Local Colour. It too is characterized by a powerful allegiance to place. Its images, metaphors, characters and thematic concerns are bound very much to the region of its setting. However, it differs from Local Colour in that these elements, though still rooted in historical time/space, somehow combine to give the impression not only of delineating the locale but of representing it (or significant aspects of it), of summing it up, of conveying the spirit of that place at a given moment in its journey through time. I think of Haliburton's *The Clockmaker*, Ringuet's *Thirty Acres*, Leacock's *Sunshine Sketches of a Little Town*, Roberts' "Tantramar Revisited", Carman's "Low Tide on Grand Pré", Roi's *The Tin Flute*, Gelinas' *Bousille and the Just*, among many. Because works of Spiritus Loci have a special representative power in regard to their region, they, unlike most of the works of Local Colour, are more likely to be of sustained interest to their regional audience over succeeding generations. They have been cherished there from the beginning. They too may initially appeal to a broader readership, depending upon the whims of the period (Leacock's *Sunshine Sketches* travelled well beyond Mariposa as a humorous piece of high order; McClelland and Stewart's Seal Book Award is currently flinging first novels into world orbit), but outside the region they are not likely to be revered as part of the general canon, certainly not for the quality that has made them special to their immediate community. Like works of Local Colour, they often have to be appropriated by a later generation who reads them again for reasons quite different from those of Local Colour. We return to and redeem, from their regional ground, works of Spiritus Loci because they give us a powerful impression of place (terrain, period, event, theme), of places so representatively rendered that we can carry them in our heads. They enter our consciousness quite differently from the specific detail of Local Colour: they tell us not so much what it was like to be there, but what it *felt like*; they become a shorthand for readers of one region to know the hearts of those in another; as metaphors for their own region, they drift free of time and space without ever leaving them. From these works, the wider community of Canadians begins to construct a map of its collective past, partly imagined and partly real. That so many works imbued with the Spirit of Place are being appropriated immediately by the general community is surely a sign of the political maturation of this country: French's *Leaving Home*, Hodgins' *Spit Delaney's Island* and the regional poetry of Suknaski, Pitman and Kroetsch are important recent examples. Some of these, having been appropriated with too much enthusiasm, may well be rejected by the next generation, but our enthusiasm is surely a sign of our need for works of Spiritus Loci as well as a testament to the abiding power of regionality as a force in literature, despite the centralizing pressures of the times.

The third distinctive type is the literature of Virtual Place. It too is grounded in time and space; it renders the local detail faithfully; it has the representative power to evoke the spirit of its region. I am thinking here of books like Buckler's *The Mountain and the Valley*, Mitchell's *Who Has Seen the Wind* and the Manawaka novels of Margaret Laurence. They were recognized and appropriated almost immediately by both the regional and general audience, and have survived beyond the first generation. Some few, like Ross's *As For Me and My House* and Ostenso's *Wild Geese* – having been overlooked in the earlier, less certain period of our nationhood – have been more recently redeemed. But all of them have been seen as qualitatively different from, say, *Cabbagetown*. Not because they may or may not be "better literature", but because they brought to us a quality beyond Local Colour and Spiritus Loci. There was about these great novels of Virtual Place an immediate power, a direct psychological appeal, a transforming energy of language, style and intention that compelled us to embrace them without qualification. Drawing power and radiance from their fidelity to the regions that spawned them, they stretched out to the general community from the bedrock of place. They travelled far because they delved down and in. (It might be argued that similar claims were made long ago for the poetry of Lampman, Carman and Roberts, but at that point in our striving towards national community we were only twenty years out of the womb and hoping to be more than a mere collocation of provinces – several of whom had not been imagined yet; we had no representative community of readers, and much of the special pleading was being done by the writers themselves. We should note, in passing, the pathetic/heroic attempts of these writers and their Canada First supporters to create by artificial insemination, as it were, a *national* consciousness through a *nationally* inspired literature. It didn't take hold then, and won't now.)

It is, then, the dimension of *virtual* place that gives works like those of Laurence and Alice Munro their unique appeal. Theirs are stories that create the illusion of a place, a virtual image of a landscape rendered in geophysical and psychological detail. From actual locales set in historical time, Manawaka and Jubilee break free of their geographical/temporal moorings; they remind us of prairie towns and Ontario hamlets, never relinquishing the tinge and tang of local detail but able at the same time to stir in us memories of *all* the small towns and rural stretches we have known or imagined in the broadloomed air of our condominiums. They give us breathing, fully rendered characters like Del Jordan and Hagar Shipley whose voices ring in our heads, whom we have conversations with, and sometimes make the measure of our own humanness. So completely realized, in regional terms, are these landscapes and the ethos they represent that even the familiar is rendered new; we can never again view even our own terrain in quite the same way. Such works are rooted in time, but not fixed there, as are their counterparts of Local Colour and Spiritus Loci. The latter may be appropriated; the former are born into us the moment we read them. As a community we cannot invent them; we merely recognize them as they come to us, and offer thanks.

Thus it is that, if we wish to grow into a genuine community, we must seek out these fundamental icons of our collective identity: rediscovering those we may have overlooked from the past and embracing those already in our midst. Fortunately they are everywhere. Among our poetry, I think of Purdy's *In Search of Owen Roblin*, Birney's *The Damnation of Vancouver*, Newlove's "The Pride", Atwood's *The Journals of Susanna Moodie*, Marshall's *The Elements*, Lee's *Civil Elegies*; among the fiction, besides those already mentioned, are Wright's *Farthing's Fortunes* and Davies' *Fifth Business*, both of which germinate in the regional loam of Ontario and move out to the battlefields of Europe and those far coigns of the world that are no longer immune from the probing of Canadian imaginations; and in drama we have the *Donnelly Trilogy*, that nine-hour claustrophobic by Reaney which focuses so relentlessly on a single time and place that it seems to burst through time itself. And many more, large or small, known or unacknowledged – all of which take hold in Local Colour, pass through Spiritus Loci towards Virtual Place, then reach for the regions of the heart.

For there is a sense in which the literature of region aspires to a fourth and more rarefied dimension. All of the major works referred to above deal with time as much as space. Not the fixed time of mere Local Colour nor that putative "timelessness" so beloved of the internationalists, but rather the magic nexus where time and space intersect, liberating both. Novels like the Manawaka tetralogy and great poems like "The Pride" allow us to see our own past – to feel it so vividly in the rhythms and in the crucible of their language – that we can sense it both for what it was, a part of the common heritage, and what it is: a mirror on the present. Because these works themselves deal with the *meaning* of time and the metaphoric implications of space, we as readers can liberate them at will from their history in order to use them, here and now, as touchstones for our own feelings. We come to know the whole world of Manawaka so well that we feel we understand something vital and secret about prairie life and values, yet at the same time we can lift up that world like a shield of ice from a pond, whole in our hands and our heart, and see through it, or in it, ourselves and our neighbours; we can set it over against the other worlds we think we know; we can even gaze through its crystal into the possibilities of the future. Literature of this stature is about the past touching the future, which is really another name for the present. Such literature, of course, must first be about *somebody's* past-future: the writer's, then a reader's, then a community of readers'. Only in this sense does it aspire to the so-called universal.

So it is that we retrieve the literature of Local Colour to fill in the details of our historical map. We turn to other works imbued by Spiritus Loci to give those details representative life and metaphoric possibility. We respond to those few masterpieces of Virtual Place with full humility to feel the past and the future touch. When this happens we must say, figuratively speaking, that they have become "timeless", acknowledging that they have moved beyond the spirit of virtual place directly into the Region of the Heart. We have let them become for us hallmarks of our own identity, endowing them with the vigour of belief, entrusting to them a part of our collective, precarious future.

I believe that this account of the regionality of our literature and its power to transform us in significant ways is neither a grandiloquent apologia nor a self-serving manifesto. Not all the literature that moves us deeply is regionally engendered (I recall Phyllis Webb's stunning *Naked Poems*, Gwendolyn MacEwan's Egyptian surrealities, or Irving Layton reinventing himself with every book); nor is it necessarily our own (I still glance at Shakespeare now and then). This has not been an argument for the exclusive virtues of literature produced by Canadian citizens. It began with a discussion of the dilemma facing Canadians as they try to imagine for themselves a continuing community of peoples sharing a common history and geography, however accidental or various these might have been. Literature has a role to play in the enterprise here as it has elsewhere. The question for us at the moment is not whether we have a literature or whether it is "any good", but rather how it may be used to give us a sense of self and community. The self-proclaimed crusade of the federalists against the infidel forces of regionalism has profound implications for how our literary works may be exploited by one side or the other. The federalists seem likely to assume that the recent proliferation of arts councils with their own mini-nationalist goals and cultural tunnel-vision are a real threat to unity. From the provincial viewpoint, the Canada Council, the Canada Studies Foundation and the colloquies of provincial Ministers of Education are looking more like a centralist plot every day. And we have writers themselves trumpeting from both sides, hurling poisoned epithets wildly across borders. My fear is that provincialism will lead to the beatification of Local Colour, with the regional idyll duly enshrined. But *Who Has Seen the Wind* will not stay put in Saskatchewan and Margaret Laurence moved to Ontario. The federalists on the other hand will end up promoting the bowdlerized version of *Two Solitudes* over *Each Man's Son* or lionizing Richard Rohmer. Neither side has been overly concerned with the true nature of regional literature – its different forms and their special uses – or its potential for contributing to the development of a community of communities, one which might someday feel comfortable in calling itself a nation.

A literature which begins in the local soil and ascends to the region of our hearts does have the power to make us feel, however tentatively, at home – not only in our own country but in a universe that renders each of us, as existential beings, speechless. And that literature is already in place.

Local Colour, Communal Consciousness, and Loretta Lynn: A Recantation

The young – stout of limb and firm of conviction – take strong stands. Sometime about the tender age of fifteen or so I remember wanting very badly to be a writer. (I also wanted very badly to play fullback for the Argos.) By nineteen I had decided in favour of the former, having not yet reached the minimum weight for Flying Wing (as it was called a long time ago). I was in university, heading unwittingly for a teaching career, studying English and basking on the beaches of the world's great literature. Secretly and furiously I was writing imitations of Keats, Shelley, and, later on, Dylan Thomas. Nonetheless, I distinctly recall, despite the absence of any respectable mention of Canadian literature (we did Am-Can), talking to a confidant about the need for a Canadian epic, or two. I suppose I had in mind a Canuckish version of *The Prelude* or *Prometheus Unbound*; in any event I thought we ought to start with the large gesture. A bit later, in graduate school, James Reaney and Carl Klinck informed me that literature had sprouted in Canada some years before my own genesis.

The point I wish to make is that despite a conventional literary upbringing, I thought of myself as a Canadian writer. What kind of Canadian though? At that time (circa 1960), I thought of nationality in terms of citizenship, ancestry (I was a Canadian; my grandparents were English, Irish and American), and history/geography (my lifelong hobbies). In selecting Champlain, LaSalle and Riel as subjects for my initial and near-disastrous forays into epic, I had nothing culturally nor psychologically profound in mind – no "message for my people" to use the current coin. By *Coppermine* (1973) and *Borderlands* (1975), however, the figures I chose had already begun to have their own way with me; but that's another story. What I did *not* count for much, in the beginning, was nationality as locale, as region, as the dialect of the heart. As a rural, small-town boy I bolted to the nearest metropolis

(Western U) and its wondrous intellectual temptations, and hurled my moth-body gratefully against its sundry torches. The language of poetry, rooted in the history and culture of England, was a form of liberation for those of us imprisoned by the regional tongue and the seemingly closed value-system it bespoke. Shakespeare didn't rob us of our birthright, he gave it back to us – in iambics.

So it seemed then; and I can still feel those original emotions through the haze of memory, though I now *see* them differently. For much happened between then and now. I continued to see myself as a Canadian poet, but the nationalness of my stance and work was becoming much more cultural and psychological. My fascination with figures from our shared history (Riel, Matonabbee, Maquina, Tecumseh) and our unexorcised landscapes (Prairies, West Coast, Barrens, Precambrian forests) continued apace. I assumed that in some way my attraction to these symbols was compulsive (it was) and more importantly was indicative of some *universally Canadian* search for identity (it may well have been, but I, as writer, had no right to think it was so). What I wasn't fully conscious of or didn't want to accept (take your pick) was that, all along, the instinct to write – to seize the symbols around one with uncontrollable compulsion and fuse them to words without regard to immediate meaning or conscious purpose (the essential, defining act of making poems) – this primary urge was, all along, propelled by my feeling for the region I had occupied for forty years and refused to call "home".

Writing about Riel and the Prairies or Maquina and Nootka Sound (not having seen either beforehand) was never a conscious attempt to be Canadian in a pseudo-psychological, cultural or (heaven forfend) archetypal sense, or to speak intentionally to a widening audience of self-confessing nationalists – despite any admissions or claims by the writer after the fact. Many of us, as writers, found it convenient to do so, perhaps were even embarrassed not to agree with enthused readers, teachers and profs so earnestly (at last) on our side. But no genuine poet chooses his subjects, topics or settings to serve ends outside himself, however tempting or compelling. The judgement of the next generation will ruthlessly weed out any of us who have been such "poetenders". What I am suggesting now, for myself and others, is that many of us, bogus and genuine, participated in the illusion that we were helping to create a national consciousness by addressing in our poetry those pan-continental concerns usually associated with nation-building. At our best and most true, however, we were contributing to an enlarged sense of community only when we were working with words and forms that grew out of our home ground.

Paradoxically (and this is where the confusion arises for both writer and reader), even when we harrowed the local soil in good faith, we needed to feel the sense of reaching out to something beyond ourselves, beyond the meanings only half-released in our words, beyond the local audience too willing to say yes. Somehow we needed to *feel* that we were, as poets, participating in a more general human enterprise. The notion of emerging nationhood is one such enlarging enterprise; it calls for an attention to what is around us and in us that goes deeper than mere enhancement of local colour. By yearning outward we are driven downward to the primary red, the annihilating black, the ineffable white. We must not fool ourselves into thinking that we can contribute to a heightening of communal consciousness – what we share as a people inhabiting these regions at this time, not excluding our political fantasies – by either decorating the multi-regional mosaic or gunning for pan-arctic themes. In this context, both the overtly national and narrowly regional poem are not relevant.

My own folly in this regard was both perverse and prolonged. As early as 1968 I began to write, alongside the historical/geographical books, a series of poems rooted in my home territory. This strain continued, culminating in *A True History of Lambton County* (1977) and *God's Geography* (1982). What I believed was happening at the time, though, was that two distinct kinds of impulse were at work: one which resulted in poems national in scope and another which prompted more personal and intimately local verse. I always believed (hoped?), of course, that both types were equally "psychological" and "universal" in appeal. Yet I persisted in feeling that they were discrete types impelled somehow by different inner needs. What I believe now is that each type is a manifestation of the same need for the poet to know his own territory – the terrain of dreams as well as the ground we colonize with our walking. Sometimes the poet reaches out for more communal, extended metaphors not to know the community beyond more intimately but to find out how far his private visions will travel; at other times he delves down to see how much of what lies below is already in him and in the wider culture of which he feels a part. His readers meet him half way: they look for the personal through his public symbols and the communal in his private ones. But *any* public symbols (historical figures, landscapes) gain poetic legitimacy only when they are psychological extensions of local knowledge, real or imagined. Conversely, poetry of mere local colour is invariably a less powerful form of verse if it is not imbued with a sense that this is knowledge whose essence can be felt by readers beyond the region through the sheer *presentation* of its detail.

If my version of Riel and his prairie has any meaning at all for future readers it will be because I knew and loved the wide spaces and infinite horizons of my home terrain: Lambton County is as flat as the Canadian dollar; Lake Huron is a saltless, magical seascape; and my childhood was haunted by Indians, actual and horrifically dreamed. And the epics I so fondly-foolishly dreamed of crafting in my salad days turned out to be only incrementally epic. In fact they have always been unalterably lyric, attached to the lyric of place they have attempted to echo, whether it be the expanse of imagined prairie or reimagined Lambton farmland, the surrogate ancestry of Maquina or the lives of my grandfathers.

Oddly enough, the event which caused me to accept the absolute primacy of the local over the national was seeing the film *Coalminer's Daughter*, the story of country singer Loretta Lynn. While it was generally praised as an exceptional film, I was still unable to account for the profound and lasting effect it had on me. The character of Loretta, her story and her songs tapped wells of unconscious feeling I could not explain in any way that made sense to me. I had always shunned country music, though surrounded by it in my youth. It represented much of what I had escaped from; it seemed, even later, to remain anti-poetic – accentuating the sentimental and the trivial, and falsely enhancing the value of local colour. But the sight of that ninety-pound, quarter-breed girl, born into the grime of poverty and numbing labour, surprising life by taking hold of it and bending it into music that shines with the innocence of first-knowing – overwhelmed and penetrated as only genuine art can. The poem I wrote a few weeks later says more about that particular experience and the general notion that the poetry of place is one of those few, marvellous and mysterious ways we get to recognize ourselves and extend that knowledge beyond us to a receptive, reciprocating community.

Song

(for Loretta Lynn)

1

From its nest in the
last uninfested
elm, the upside-down orchard
oriole bends her body into
song the
incipient dusk
momentarily hesitates
then rides upon

Everywhere the trees succumb
to the featureless gloom –

only with you a hum of
waferous bones, skull
ringing like a Sunday
belfry, throat taut
as a lover's tuning fork,
without design or artifice
against the malignant night
fling
   your lyric of light

2

The image I hold of you
is not Nashville –

I see you at thirteen already dreaming
music out of your father's tarred lungs
music out of the misery of your mother's eyes
music out of ruptured hills the sun
still tints green with memory

music out of the territorial dialect –
the vowels stretched and rounded
to meet the dream your forebears
brought to these speechless valleys,
the consonants hoarded, honed, brandished
against Yankees, revenuers, carpetbaggers,
McCoys, company men, and all the do-gooding
social reformers hell bent to flatten every
accent between Goose Bay and Butcher Holler

and making

music out of your own splintered virginity
music out of a child's body pummelled by love
out of a nine-month belly bevelled by love
out of little-girl grace transformed by love
into song

3

The image I make of you
is this:

you are Keats' nightingale
swallowed by song
you keep history and
innocence as pure as
Ruth's pristine cry,
though the words be
our own currency

Words we share
the blame for, use
to disguise history
disparage innocence

words your voice
remind us of
carried intact as the
oriole's aboriginal
stammer on the
evening air

words that tear
your girl's face
into age, care
little for the love
we bring to heal
you with, spare
no flesh in their
foraging for the future.

But even now
you smile from memory
the song rises from itself
appropriates bone bent flesh
and stuns with its
juggernaut of joy.

Homage to the Past-Future

1

Although the Group-of-Seven landscapes now seem dated to us (certified cliché by seven Canadian banks), when we look at them in light of their nineteenth-century counterparts, the question we ask is not "Are these authentic responses?" but rather "What took them so long to emerge?" The refusal to see what is in front of us, the tendency to impose acquired, comfortable forms on to those that may be inherent in the objects threatening to penetrate our vision – these exigencies are not unique to Canadians. The structures which are enclosed precariously within landscapes new to our experience and which the artist is always poised to liberate, are universally dangerous. They have the potential to disrupt our quotidian comforts simply because they seem novel; more significantly, though, they may also be familiar, reminding us of states and feelings we prefer to keep lodged in the darkest rooms of our dreams. Novelty by itself might discomfit; the shock of the new-in-the-old can dismay. It is not surprising, then, that in a country which has literally more alien landscapes and seemingly uninhabitable spaces than most nations, our artists would be cautious in their approach.

From the outset, space has been the overwhelming question not only for our painters (to whose art it is at least intrinsic) but for our writers as well. For the latter, however, space is not necessarily a welcome challenge. For novelists, for example, gazing at the prairies and trying hard to believe in horizons, an extra nominative and descriptive burden is placed on a story-telling art that is essentially temporal and psychological. Sinclair Ross and W.O. Mitchell – and the host of prairie writers who have followed – have quite understandably focussed on the various and complex relationships between man-in-his-village and the setting-which-besets-him. The landscape, or lack of it, must then be described through the confrontations, literal and psychological, that man experiences with it: journeys through it, retreats from it, garrisons against it, epiphanies and catastrophes within it. At all costs the human scale must be preserved. Moreover, the particular landscapes we have inherited (it's not *our* fault our forebears beached us here) – prairie, bush, ancient mountain, pre-cambrian shield, sea- and snow-scape – are not only spatially awesome, they are shot through with the terrors of cosmic time. Denizen and artist alike are confronted by dinosaur bones, millennial firs, volcanic rock, stone-age neighbours, glacial alluvia, and four discrete, earth-wrenching seasons. Everywhere, even in our illusory, floral cities, we are reminded of time's depth and our own insignificance. How then do we write, with any ease, of these cosmopolitan concerns considered by other societies to be the hallmark of contemporary man? To a Czech or Parisian our continuing obsession with trees, mountains and aboriginals (*Lost in the Barrens* is still the most popular adolescent novel) must seem anachronistic, perhaps even childishly perverse.

It is neither. The Canadian imagination has still not worked through the spatial/temporal challenges of our omnipresent landscape (and of course the deep psychological correlatives it engenders), despite the brilliant fiction of Ross, Buckler, Roy, Kroetsch, Mitchell, Carrier, Laurence and others. We have come a long way towards facing the questions of Canadian/historical man in *this* time/space, but we have not yet examined the latter on their own terms, as they are in their *being* and *coexistence* with us. That is a challenge more readily addressed by the poet.

The poem is at its best at the lyric or epic extremes. The epic mode has the broad sweep, rhythmic grandeur and generosity of detail to describe, to elevate, and to approximate the scope of centuries and vistas. Traditionally the epic has been hero-centred; Pratt, for example, gives us some of the same egocentric/cinemascopic experiences as our novelists in his *Brébeuf* – European man in the primordial world – with the additional heightening effects of verse rhythm and extension over time. Other poems, though, like *The Cachelot*, *The Great Feud* and parts of *The Titanic* hint at the potential of epic for exploring the primordial from its own perspective. The lyric, on the other hand, can render brief and powerful psychological states of relationship between man and landscape (Birney's "Bushed", Atwood's "Progressive Insanities"); its 'time' is both dramatically focussed in the present (moving to what Langer calls "virtual future") and at the same time universal in implication. Paradoxically, though, it is limited in its capacity to simulate extended movement over time and space.

What we have begun to see, starting as early as Crawford (epic) and Scott (lyric) and developing steadily over the last forty years in particular, is the attempt by our writers to use the more flexible resources of poetry to probe man's psychic interaction with landscape by extending it beyond the descriptive accounts in our fiction to encompass the more universal aspects of man in time/space: dream, continuity, genesis, mortality, ontology, epistemology. Purdy's Eskimo poems (lyric mode) and Newlove's "The Pride" stand as touchstones for this wider movement. What the poets have been doing, consciously or otherwise, is discovering what the confrontation with landscape – the *living-through-it*, as it were – will reveal about the very linguistic structures needed to render it in a way we feel (we can never know) is closer to its own state of being. And since our prairies and barrens run beyond the eye's ken and any conventional apprehension of time, the traditional epic with its Aristotelian beginning and end and the domestic lyric with its tempting illusion of timelessness will not long stay in place. New ways of opening up the epic without sacrificing its characteristic length and rhythm, and of prolonging the present-tense power of the lyric over time/space, had to be found.

What, then, are the forms that will best render in some manageable way this Leviathan we must try to swallow if we are to get on with our lives? And what, if they can be found, will these forms do to the language of art itself? To the minds and spirits of those who deploy it and to those who dare respond? Ultimately the business of art and literature is not merely a formalistic game; it is even more than a reciting, however faithfully, of our encounters with history and the environment. It is, at heart, a cyclic drama in which we spin words out of the cocoon of our communal dream, watch them assume character, contention, temporary resolution before they betray and are replaced by the dream-speaking beings who prompted them. And when we gaze *out there* we find signs of other kinds of future-dreaming; and then our words may strive to make contact, arrest, contain or surrender: inner dream touching the outer, past reaching for the future, *I* becoming *am*. Poetry is the place where we expect to see language breaking down under pressure from the dreamer and the thing imposing itself from without – breaking down and re-collecting so that the reader, if he is susceptible and lucky, may look both ways and feel simultaneously both the results and the process. It is of course the language, the poetic itself, that both represents the experience and renders it. Moreover, it must do so in a way which does not draw undue attention to itself since it is the medium, the means-in-the-end, and never the end *per se*.

2

The foregoing are some of the thoughts and feelings I had after reading Jon Whyte's *Homage, Henry Kelsey*. This book-length poem is, according to its author's statements in the afterword and its own self-evident effects, an epic. Whyte, a prairie poet, sets out to do a number of things with the story of Henry Kelsey, the first white man to venture onto the Barren Lands (a prairie analogue?) and then claim it for the Hudson's Bay Company. Whyte seems intrigued that nineteen-year-old Kelsey was the first of our breed to see this alien, ancient, other-worldly landscape and capture it with a version of our own dialect. In fact Kelsey left us both a series of doggerel couplets and a set of journal entries, each of which in its own way provides a record of the man and what he saw. Working from this scant evidence, Whyte reconstructs the journey (two of them it appears) in very special terms. He lets Kelsey speak through his own verses, but these are scattered, out of order, throughout the five parts of the book (and reproduced verbatim in an appendix); he fleshes out Kelsey's narrative and commentary by adding new couplets and first-person poetic accounts of several sorts; he also salutes Kelsey directly in a post-modern voice. More importantly, though, Whyte goes well beyond recreating Kelsey and his adventure, beyond the usual re-dramatization of European man in alien setting (though that motif is present), beyond the enticing exploitation of Kelsey-Barren Lands as symbol or correlative. Whyte is obsessed by the landscape itself, by the beauty and terror of its existence. He wants to know it *as it was* for Kelsey in his time, for us in ours, and for all between. He needs to know, therefore, more about the language and forms that Kelsey used to cope with it then. He wants to re-experience, re-work, re-write them; and, quite naturally, he wants in the course of achieving these aims to find out what his own linguistic resources can accomplish by looking straight at the object and trying to apprehend it on its own fierce terms. The result is an 'epic' structure that is discontinuous, multiform, ideogrammatic and narrative by turns, rooted in the field-theory of discourse and in structuralist poetics.

Besides the epigraphs from Levi-Strauss and George Steiner, numerous statements through the five parts of the book point to the central ideological concerns of the poet:

locus of history about
a centre
a vision forming landscape
a manner of seeing
in the current of circumstance
(p. 11)

Nothing is knowable   except uncertainty
(p. 28)

The river flows both ways
(p. 30 and *passim*)

Time, depth and distance fall away...
The muteness of my mouth where language
falls away from me
(p. 43)

form and idea
collide and collapse
(p. 45)

take away the tree and what remains is
poetry
(p. 62)

the universeis free
limitedbut unbound
horizoned but infinite
(p. 67)

Sphere : a way of thinking
Sphere : a manner of perception location...

Sphere of the eye Sphere of the world
together a lens each focussing
the other
(p. 67)

And so on.

In the collision and contiguities of landscape, personae (Kelsey, poet, various beasts and vegetable creatures), dialects, and signs, Whyte discovers the paradoxes noted above: the finite in the infinite, the reversibility and relativity of time/space, the grip and release of language itself, the implosion of form and content – culminating in a fresh "manner of seeing". Kelsey's 'story' and the Barrens, then, are not the subject of the poem so much as parts of its meaning. "Simultaneity" and "synchronicity" (terms used in the poem) are in a sense both subject and outcome. Whyte tries to *render* these abstractions in a number of ways, most of them at one point or another stunningly successful:

(1)

The words of Kelsey himself occasionally startle with their clarity jutting through the doggerel or hackneyed journal-entry:

For Every man maketh his own songs
by vertue of what he dreams of...

& so by their singing
will pretend to know at the firmament of heaven is
made of...

So likewise another has told me
Yet he had been so near to ye sun at ye going down
yt he could take hold of it when it Cut ye Horizon

(2)

Whyte, taking up the persona of Kelsey, is able to describe certain vivid events as Kelsey might have imagined them and as he (Whyte) is now able to:

> The wind is singing in a woman's voice,
> dark and mysterious is the wind;
> the land lies fertile yielding to me,
> the sun is silver and the sky is bright,
> and I am called by the wind to the land,
> the wind which is singing in a woman's voice
> and the land that lies like a woman lying
> beneath the sun which burns in the air
> (p. 38)

A refinement of this technique occurs when Whyte adopts both Kelsey's persona and his rhyming couplet technique. Here he is able to expand the descriptive detail of the Barrens and suggest the extension in time of the poetic form itself, its capacity for stasis and change.

> At the last of summer's false return the bison
> clouded the plain turned sky unto horizon
> and at their burrows' entrances the squirrels
> awaited licks of wind, dustdevil whirls,
> to sully the yellow, golden, pale blue flowers
> of asters, ragweed, bergamot in hours
> drying, reseeding this land "of good report,"
> so pale, once bountiful, unlike the fort
> I left in spring's onset to undertake
> this inland journey for my masters' sake.
> (p. 24)

Going one step further, Whyte at times adopts Kelsey's couplets and even his conventions of spelling and abbreviation. Here he replicates the order and events of the original Kelsey poem (about ninety lines in length), adding some detail but mostly "improving" the original through rhythmic variety and enjambement. Thus Whyte's re-living/reworking the Kelsey experience, like the Etomomi River in part two, "runs both ways" towards re-envisioned content and re-assembled form.

> Pitcht to ye outtermost Edge of ye woods
> Where y^t ye silver haired Great Bear broods
> *His skin to gett I have used all* y^e *ways I can*
> *He is mans food & he makes food of man*
> *His hide they would not me it preserve*
> *But said it was a god & they should starve**
> Neither white nor black like ye common Bear
> But more like unto y^t our English Hare
> Also Buffillo like the English ox their horns
> Unlike those y^t to N^otharward are born
> (p. 54)
> * italics are Kelsey's words

(3) Throughout the book Whyte describes in long-line narrative-descriptive verse aspects of the Barrens, its creatures and ecosystem which interest him as a Canadian and a Westerner, and from the perspective of a sojourner; in brief he becomes *Kelsey now.*

> Hail, Kelsey, come: the land is not barren,
> land of little sticks, caribou lichen, musketers only:
> come to the land: the land is not barren,
> the land that is mused, is browsed, is fused
> by mooseways over, among, between, and through
> the muskrat-slickened banks of oozing mud,
> its list aboil, aswarm with mosquitoes,
> the must of melting and dispersing such a wonder
> of flying, biting, cloud turmoiling things;
> come to the land: the land is not barren;
> the glaciers' scores on the rusty rock reveal
> that life withdrew but has returned;
> come, Kelsey, come to the land.
> (p. 12)

(4) Here and there we find, as well, a few objectively narrated accounts of Kelsey's movements, his past in England, his tiffs with Hudson's Bay officials, *et al.* None of these is distinguished enough to quote; in fact they seem decidedly out of place for the most part, reminding us too much of the 'story as content' in a dead-handed way. (This obsession with naming, with filling in the details – in a country thin with mythology – has plagued many poets before Whyte.)

(5) More effectively Whyte adopts the personae of various creatures whose essential being is often powerfully portrayed. These personified fauna and flora also act as radiant ideograms for the paradoxes of time and eternity, finite and indefinite space, essence as "thing-ness", the word as flesh escaping flesh, and so on. Here, for example, is the pleistocene musk-ox at the moment of its individual death:

> Sweat flecks the tawny hide, urging
> the ecstasy the buck dies in, surging
> ecstasy crumbling on its legs splaying,
> slaughter's dreary darkness replacing
> the surgent rapture.
>
> The Larynx tightens; the word is drawn back;
> before the utterance is thrown, the breath is drawn;
> the heart's cords and the hand's tendons tighten;
> song brims in the tension of silence.
>
> Let my song fly; the arrow is true.
> (p. 48)

Whyte's handling of assonance, enjambment and multi-layered imagery is nowhere better illustrated. The same versatility and dexterity is shown later in part five where the poet becomes the Barrens' stunted, surviving, triumphant tree.

> If thou wouldst me define,
> seek the blast that has thee bent,
> seek the element in which thou grew,
> seek the old supporting the new;

number the rings, tell the annuli of growth...
look to the gnarls of the roots;
look to the shape of the insistent wind;
look with a persistent mind.
(p. 63)

Equally evocative presentations are made for the bear (astral and mammalian), the herd-instinct of the musk-ox and for winter-as-wolf.

(6) There is more. Probing ever more deeply into the forms of the landscape's projection of time/space, Whyte struggles to find ways of approximating its simultaneity and synchronicity. He comes up with a format (modelled, the poet tells us, on Octavio Paz' "Sun Stone"). It consists of setting up two and occasionally three columns of verse so that the reader may read down each column, serially, as well as across the spaces.

aloneremembering
the lost aimlessly
in circles stumbling
come upon their own fear snaring themselves
fatally in a question
(p. 20)

The poem on the left makes its own sense, as does the one on the right, complementary versions of the same experience. Moreover, we may read the columns as part of a single large poem whose phrases are marked by space; in this case the spaces interject themselves into the meaning of the passage which is itself about being lost in them. Whyte works many variations on this technique, not all of them successful: but the intent is always clear: to break up our customary predilections, to get us thinking about both time and space (we read the variants – one, two, three; reverse the order; and yet are kept ever aware of their *position* and relative *contiguity*). Several of these field-compositions are simultaneously chants and charts which are used effectively as rousing close-outs for major sections of the book.

3

All of these discrete "ways of seeing" are not quite as randomly presented as the foregoing might suggest. The poem is divided into five parts, plus an interlude and epilogue. Each part, as its title implies, centres on a major symbol (ideogram really, because the object rendered stands for both itself and the other things). Part one is called "List", focussing on the need for *naming* the apparent blankness Kelsey first sees (making lists) and the necessity of shifting perspective in order to see things anew (the listing of the voyager's canoe). Connected closely with "list" is the word "ungava" as a sort of rune or magic word lying in "lee of the eye" waiting to be unveiled when the right "manner of seeing" is achieved. From the opening phrases of the poem, Whyte makes it clear that ungava is a sign-word for the focussing /liberating synthesis of experience he and Kelsey (and the voyaging reader) are about to discover; and what-is-more unagava is to be found in *our own mind.* Around ungava and listing, then, the poet reconstructs the journey not by narrating it but, as we have seen, by presenting its parts – events, sightings, insightings, icons, delineations – in multiformal array. Part two, "Etomomi", is built in similar fashion around the image of the two-way river: the journey out is the journey back, a circle not a straight line, etc. We also get our first look at the musk-ox: on the move, retracing his eons-old trek across the earth's most ancient face. But the dominant symbol here is the journey itself, whose true nature lies in the river's circularity, to be revealed only when the illusory terrors of space, of light and shadow, day and night have been exorcized. Part of the exorcism involves the acceptance of the right role of language in describing things as they are, without appropriation.

> language is a vehiclethe universe decrees
> for its description   creating spaces
> for another space   to exist
> silence between utterances   in space
> in which are actsacts begetting facts
> in which words form   totem, factotum
> fact, act, fiction   the thing made
> in space   a journey made
> made   journeyman's creation
> time
> (p. 32)

Part three is "Nivation" – literally the growth beneath the snow and symbolically the sensuous world that shapes our dreams, the datum out of which ideas rise and then die when the vital connection is severed. The central image here is the musk-ox in winter, beset by wolves and finding safety in the instinct for the protective ring and in the in-tuneness with the timeless wind. Into this primal order of things blunders the white man, killing the ox and, figuratively, his own link with real time. The experience, however, proves cathartic as these final lines in part three suggest:

> It is a beginning;
> the wind is singing,
> fire is dying:
> the voice of the land is the wind
> the wind is the voice of the land, and
>
> when you have heard the wind and its
> singing,
> you shall have begun to understand.
> (p. 43)

Whyte's deliberate anti-narrative approach is clear here, for this 'growing' experience is set *after* the epiphanies already achieved in part two. We are simply looking at the total experience from yet another, unchronologic angle (serves us right for expecting the usual order of things!).

The interlude "Dreambearer" and the related fourth part, "Flensing", extend the range of perspectives on, and available metaphors for, seeing time and space anew. The death of an individual ox (quoted above from page 48) and a detailed report of its gutting and flensing suggest again the necessity for stripping away, for seeing into the forms below the surface of things. The slaughter images, as always interrupted by fragments from the journals and pseudo-journals, are balanced here by a sequence on the bear who is both beast and constellation. This section concludes with several descriptions of Kelsey's encounter with the aborigines, finishing up with an epiphanous smoking of the peace-pipe.

Part five, "Arbor", takes the tree with its rings, seasonal fletchings, recurrent seeding (earlier the tree was equated with a poem) and launches into a sort of coda or grand finale in which the major *ideas* are unarrestingly made explicit:

> ...myth makes history meaningful
> while making of it something else
> (p. 66)

Finally, the epilogue, "The Scab", zeroes in on Kelsey's journal, the ephemeral nature of all writing and its paradoxical permanence, in and out of time.

> The story continues, the story is ended.
> The story continues, "The story is ended..."
> The story continues
> (p. 73)

4

Whyte's poem is a valiant effort to explore and represent a particular Canadian space and time – a part of that North that haunts us overhead and underneath, one which we apparently met and conquered about three hundred years ago. The journals are there to prove it; so is the Hudson's Bay Company. But the Barrens, as Whyte knows and wishes us to know, are neither conquerable nor empty. He has accepted the task of naming its parts, without precondition; he has ransacked our language and our poetics to let as much of its sundering forms show through (as much as we can take) and remind us about the actual nature of the spaces we purport to inhabit.

As my analysis has implied, large parts of the effort are successful. As an epic poem, however (and Whyte's own remarks make this claim for it), *Homage, Henry Kelsey* does not work as well as it might have. In part, the failure is due simply to a slackening of poetic power or control. Some of the more descriptive and ruminative sections go on too long without adding much to the meaning of a section or the poem as a whole. These lapses are all the more obvious because some of the ideogrammatic parts and three-column sets are overwhelmingly effective in *rendering* the idea-in-the-thing.

Another, more indigenous, difficulty is Whyte's insistence on getting all of Kelsey's 'story' interwoven with the central encounters, real and imagined. Part four is severely weakened by overly extensive iterations from Kelsey's doggerel, too much 'flat' description of the skinning of the musk-ox, and a mere listing or naming over of the local flora and fauna (the relevance of this latter is evident but is nonetheless ponderous reading). Quite often the field-compositions are so beautiful (where listing is enlivened by rhythm and horizontal-vertical tensions) and true that we would prefer large spaces to be left in the text so that we could rest between rounds. On occasion Whyte even diminishes the power of these sections by going over the same ground from a more mundane angle. In his afterword Whyte mentions that the book was written in separate parts over a period of ten years or so, and this may explain the unevenness of the final editing: it's hard to cut material that has been born out of such extended, loving struggle.

In addition, and more seriously, I question the over-explicitness of the idea so baldly stated on pages 66-68. For example:

> Given: a sphere
> point moving locus
>
> Wherever the point is on the sphere, it is the centre of
> the circle
> at the centre of many circles
>
> Given: a sphere
> point still locus
> The radius of the circle equals a radius of the sphere
> (p. 66)
>
> Circle: a plane of intersection of two spheres
> a way of thinking, a mode of perception
> Circle: the intersection of a sphere and plane
> the volumetric intersection of a pair of
> spheres: a lens
> (p. 67)

On the oblate disc
formed of two spherical sections
ringed by the circle's perfection
(recall, now, the ringed muskoxen)
aware of the dish-disc apposite
which forms the boundary
(p. 67)

"Recall, now, the ringed muskoxen" is particularly offending. After all, we have *lived through* the 'list' of perspectives, making our own way as best we can towards ungava. To be told what it is we have just reassembled for ourselves through the glinting two-way river of Whyte's poetry at its finest is an anti-climax we don't deserve. Indeed, if large parts of the whole were not as successful as they patently are, we might be inclined, in light of the above, to suspect that the ideas therein did not *emerge* from the re-lived Kelsey experience but were, alas, *grafted* on to it. This sort of suspicion has occasionally been raised by others in connection with some post-modernist, structuralist-inspired verse.

We cannot forget that the purpose of form in poetry – whether it be post or ante anything – is initially to call attention to itself (the desideratum of dislocation and fresh perspective) and then as quickly as possible make itself both window and mirror. For example, my initial response to Whyte's three-column field-composition was "What's this? Do I read across? Down? Both ways? In any particular order?" I tried each alternative, carefully and in turn, until meanings started jumping off the page. By the second such encounter I was at home with the basic technique so that I read for meaning *through* the formal demands, feeling equally the imperatives of the stretching devices and the full weight of the landscape experienced in ways I had hitherto not imagined. When a technique of any kind continues to call attention to itself or fails to render more meaning than the sum of its tropes – whether its essential nature be novel or familiar, experimental or conventional – then the poetry fails as poetry. The structuralist trap (form *as* content) is no less tempting or disastrous than that of any other set of poetics; it is merely different. These lines that conclude part five are worth more than the four pages of laboured, self-centred tautologies which precede them:

until in the specula,
in the discovery of the aspiring breath,
vaporous, spirant breath,
the soft wind singing the primitive,
the archaic words seething on the brim
of the old leather pot in which the hot stones
are dropped

words pulse like birds pulse in the pulse arrow
singing pulse like
the heart pulse in the body pulse
the rhythmpulse   the wind pulse
till in the heat of your transformation   pulse

all and all else
escapes inertia

little matters

will
(p. 71)

Here Whyte has drawn from the ancient reservoirs of poetic convention – rhythm, repetition, consonance, referential imagery – to convey ideas, feelings and the feeling-in-ideas. The passage as a whole is marvellously balanced by the controlling/contrastive c- and p-sounds, and even the apparent total escape at the end is hauntingly constrained by the enclosing rhyme of "will" and "until". From the modern and post-modern repertoire, the poet takes the word-itself-as-object ("pulse") and the new rhythms permitted by spatial display, and recreates the energy of the earth's word-beat pumping through space and time to some momentary release. Here indeed is the "old supporting the new", a poetry where "specula" and that "old leather pot" reside in harmony.

When I return to *Homage, Henry Kelsey* (and I shall quite often), it will not be as a field-discourse version of epic. Rather I shall approach the book as I would a collection of Al Purdy's: coming back again and again to the same poems – the ones that glow in the dark like polished Eskimo carvings sculpted from the language of my contemporaries.

5

I began by talking about space and painters. *Homage, Henry Kelsey* quite appropriately is complemented by a series of original ink drawings by the noted Canadian artist, Dennis Burton. How much easier it is for the painter to render the gestalt configuration of burnished sky, sun-shattered barren-grass, and the infinite stretch and recession of primary colour. It is a tribute to Jon Whyte that the best of his own word-chants sit comfortably beside Burton's etched and shimmering clarities. Together they make this hymn to the past-future an exceptional artistic experience.

Reference

Jon Whyte, *Homage, Henry Kelsey*. Winnipeg: Turnstone Press, 1981.

The Coherence of Consonance in Poetry

1

There has been a great deal of critical writing about sound values, metre and rhythm in poetry. It is often a very erudite and rarefied excursion. One may reasonably ask what is left to be said on the subject. My own perspective on the topic is threefold: as a practising poet, a full-time teacher, and more recently as a visiting artist-in-the-schools reading my work and enticing young students to compose verse of their own. The particular aspects of the subject I wish to explore, from this three-legged stance, are 1) the role of the sounds-in-words as a principal factor (for some poets on some occasions) in the compositional process itself, and 2) if the influence of sound structure on the emergence of meaning during the genesis of a poem *is* significant, the possibility that the reader's responses to that structure may have to be adjusted accordingly. Put another way, understanding the signal system presented by patterns of sound (I will use the generic term *consonance* to refer to all types of meaningful repetition of consonants and vowels) should add to the pleasures and insights we associate with reading verse. Moreover, those general readers who shy away from poetry because its landscape is less domestic than that of fiction or simply because it is 'too hard to read' may be given one of the keys to its comprehension.

We begin by reviewing briefly some of the conventional ways in which readers have interpreted consonance:

(1) Strongly marked consonance – rhymes, refrains, repetition of key words – helps the reader to locate and focus on 'chunks' of the text which in turn clarify the shape and intensity of thought and feeling. Rhymed stanzas, quatrains, summary couplets, and thematic refrains work in this manner.

(2) More subtle forms of consonance – alliterative and assonantal effects – highlight or draw attention to word-groupings whose meaning is crucial to the interpretation; that is, certain key phrases are 'shaped

to the ear' through concentrated and novel clusters of sound so that we take special note of them.

(3) Sound effects of all kinds in combination with rhythm and/or metre are often said to provide orchestration or a sort of melodic accompaniment to the main 'tune' of the thought (the semantic meanings). Critics have spoken of sombre tones, base and treble effects, contrastive consonant patterns, even dark and light vowels. Milton's is an organ-voice, Sappho's a melancholy lute, and so on.

(4) Most frequently, of course, the marriage of sound and sense is seen as onomatopoeia or imitative harmony. In the most general sense onomatopoeia includes some aspects of the previous effects, but its most special application is reserved for so-called 'echoic' effects. Satan's *s*'s hiss their way through passages of *Paradise Lost*, and every schoolchild knows that the *crack* of a bat or the *twitter* of a bird is a superior way of representing the reality entailed. But as Archibald MacLeish has pointed out, (in Poetry and Experience) the number of purely echoic words in English is very small, so that to speak of onomatopoeia in this restricted form is to limit one's analysis to a minuscule percentage of all the possible effects available. Further, MacLeish exposes the fallacy of attributing *independent* meanings to any sounds before the sense is well understood. Even when the musical effects of a poem are concentrated and dominant – embedded in powerful rhythms and closed forms as in Hopkins or Dylan Thomas – they cannot be assigned definite connotations (happy/sad, bright/nostalgic) in the same manner as a melody, say, played on a harp will strike a common emotional chord in listeners. The poet, MacLeish maintains, can alter the sounds of words no further than the sense allows.[6] However, once we have been alerted to the semantic import of image and statement in a poem, sound and sense become interwoven; then the ear does distinguish significant repetitions, patterns and clusterings that shape, support and highlight our response to the meaning-as-a-whole.

With the limitations of onomatopoeia recognized, it is safe to conclude that the conventional role of sound – outlined above – is a *supporting* and *enhancing* one. It is the *structuring, connective* power, particularly of consonance, that is less well understood and that I wish now to explore in more detail.

First it is necessary to point out that in any critical analysis of poetic technique a certain mutuality of interest is usually assumed between reader and writer. If the reader finds that the consonance in a poem replicates in its own domain the 'sense' of an image pattern, he infers that the poet intended such congruent felicities (the intricacies of intentionalist questions notwithstanding). This is the normal relationship which obtains between composer and interpreter, part of the rhetorical contract that makes the enjoyment of literature possible. Secondly, I will focus on consonance – *the significant repetition of similar phonemes* (consonants and vowels internally or initially placed, stressed or unstressed) – because it seems to appear naturally in the compositions of both sophisticated and naive poets (rhyme and conventional alliteration often being taught or force-fed to the latter by their instructors). Moreover, the *predictive*, *generative* potential of consonance, as we shall see further on, may well prove to be the most important compositional feature in the writer's repertoire, and hence, if a poet's intentions become by mutual agreement transposed to a reader's legitimate inferences, an equally salient aspect of how we ought to read poetry. Thirdly, I will illustrate the role of consonance in the composing process by referring to several poems: one by a pre-eminent practitioner (Emily Dickinson), one which I wrote myself (hardly pre-eminent but providing an opportunity for me to examine the process from inside), and finally two sets of poems by naive, untutored poets writing their first poems ever. (The fact that one of these latter happens to be my daughter does not I hope make her any less typical than the hundreds of other students who have composed their first poems during my workshops in schools; rather, it means that I can verify more confidently the 'naive' circumstances of the poem's composition.)

2

Apparently with no surprise
To any happy flower,
The frost beheads it at its play
In accidental power.

The blond assassin passes on,
The sun proceeds unmoved
To measure off another day
For an approving God.

In this justly admired poem, Emily Dickinson is questioning the role of her own Christian God and this murderous little scene in which the indifference of the natural world appears repugnant to any human onlooker. Even the victim apparently conspires with its own killer while an approving God of some kind looks impassively on. The irony of the metaphors – "*beheads* it at its *play*", "*blond* assassin" – and the double entendres in "apparently", "happy", "accidental" (is the Latin verb 'to kill' being echoed here?), and "unmoved" convey both the horror felt by the poet/observer and the central paradox at the poem's core: how can such horrific beauty be part of the same divine scheme for both Nature and Man? Is, indeed, there only one God? If not, then the one directing this drama seems infinitely more powerful and vastly more indifferent than He who gave us the compassion to feel what Emily does in writing this poem. More terrifyingly, the whole procedure, endlessly and ominously repeated, may be utterly random ("*any* flower", "happy", "accidental", even "apparently"). And so on.

The *supporting* role of sound values in all this is self-evident. The consonance of *a* and *s* in "assassin passes" hisses its villainy in our ears. The masculine falling rhythms and plosive sounds of "in accidental power" reflect the awesome strength and indifference of the divinely sanctioned executioner. In contrast, the shorter words and bumptious rhythm used to describe "any happy flower...at its play" suggest the innocence, in human terms, of the victim.

Beyond these customary supporting and enhancing effects, however, lies a more important use of sound, and of consonance in particular. The structure of the poem itself appears to be built around a single set of interrelated sounds, a set which reflects as well the prevailing paradox of feeling and idea in the poem: attraction-revulsion, beauty-death, dominance-helplessness and randomness-design. "Apparently" is a key-signature, as it were, for the subsequent deployment of the consonant *p* and its cognate *b*. "Surprise" picks up the motif in a more muffled way and signals, more strongly, the start of the *s*-pattern. Immediately, "apparently" and "surprise" are linked in our mind by sound so that their sense, taken together, foreshadows two interconnected themes: the ambivalent nature of the ensuing actions and reactions and the shock felt by the persona who is about to question things even if the flowers are not. "Frost" continues, unobtrusively here, the *s*-pattern, which gathers force progressively through "behead*s* *it* at *its* play" (with modulations involving *t* and *i*) and "accidental" to the major statement in "a*ss*a*ss*in pa*sses*" and echoes in "pro*c*eed*s*" and "mea*s*ure". More than onomatopoeia is at work here. As a structural, *bridging* mechanism operating directly upon a receptive ear, this consonance pattern compels us to link, semantically, the implicit question in "*s*urpri*s*e" with the awesome power of the "fro*s*t" (playful old Jack) and "a*ss*a*ss*in". Similarly, the "*s*un proceed*s*" is connected to this pattern of events, and compromised not only because it is said to be "unmoved" but also because, if we are following the chaining of these words through the coherence of their sounds poetically deployed, "sun" is inescapably linked to "assassin" and "surprise". At the same time, Emily provides, as a counterpoint to this latter chain, the *p*/*b*-pattern introduced in "apparently": "ha*pp*y", "*b*eheads", "*p*lay", "*p*ower" and "*p*roceeds" (introducing also the related minor *d*-pattern of "behea*d*s", "acci*d*ental" and "procee*d*s". Onomatopoeically, these sounds add an appropriate sense of weight and dominance, but further effects are achieved when we see that the *p*/*b*-pattern initially referred to the victim – it's the flower who is a*pp*arently not sur*p*rised while at its ha*pp*y *p*lay – but is abruptly taken over by the executioner ("*b*eheads") who is fully revealed as a "*b*lond" assassin who "*p*roceeds unmoved" (note the marvellous closing finality provided by the consonance in "bl*on*d" and "*on*" and its later variation in "su*n*", "*un*moved" and "G*o*d"). The assassin is attractive, as the flower was; this feeling is conveyed by the image of blondness alone, but the coupling effects described above not only reinforce the irony of a beautiful murderer *per se* but add the notion that victim and victor share the *same* qualities, are part of a *single* scheme of things: slaughtering and being slaughtered are, as it were, versions of the same experience. And it is the consonance here which draws our attention to this notion and to the unrelenting questions and mixed feelings it raises for Emily and for us.

In like fashion, we can now see how much more meaning is carried by the closing line "For an approving God". With "a*pp*roving" we are compelled to draw this deity into the whole complex of action and feeling initiated by "a*pp*arently" and carried through the succeeding changes rung on the *p*/*b*-motif. He is not only an indifferent onlooker (one interpretation of the line) but also – by reference to the coherence of consonance – a full participant in the drama. Indeed, if we are following the way in which consonance helps to direct us to fresh meaning, the sounds in "God" itself remind us of "bl*on*d", "*on*" (a typical Dickinson rhyme), "acci*d*ental", "procee*d*s" and "unmove*d*". And perhaps most significantly, the coupling of "approving" and "apparently" through consonance suggests that although the latter word initially and syntactically modifies only the flower's lack of surprise, it brings similar qualification to bear on God's apparent approval. That is to say, the powerfully implied questions Emily raises about the flower's behaviour are carried over to God's as well, urging us to see the poem's last line as an assertion, a condemnation, a painfully ironic comment and a life-and-death, ontological question. In this particular instance, consonantal pattern and its associating effects broaden and deepen the meaning set in motion by the numerous other tropes, not excluding, course, the echoic and highlighting functions of sound.

I am not suggesting for a moment that the kind of nit-picking analysis displayed above is the way we habitually ought to read poetry. Metaphors, images, conventional tropes, finely-crafted statements and the generic features of verse are major means to meaning and interpretation. What I am postulating, and what this overly technical exegesis is intended to illustrate, is that, along with these latter instruments, consonance and related sound values can be more than supportive or highlighting devices, more than aesthetic features embellishing the true grit of semantic import, and certainly more than the delights of occasional imitative harmony. Consonance shares in all of these but I suspect that it goes further to the roots of poetic composition and interpretation than has been generally recognized. As the foregoing analysis implies, appropriately deployed by a master of the craft, consonance leads us to read across or through or beyond the kind of coherence established by the grammar, by rhetorical and generic convention, or by patterns of image and metaphor. It causes us to link words and phrases, observe progression and associate objects, feelings and ideas *not otherwise fully implied by the other conventions*. Without the latter, of course, it cannot work, any more than an image pattern operates outside of the norms of syntax (we supply them if the poet doesn't), but that is not to say that consonance merely enhances what is already there. The coherence of consonance always has the potential to add new meaning to the conglomerate of meanings in a poem. When used in this way it may be called a discrete kind of coherence, one which is without question unique to verse, distinguishing it absolutely from prose of any type. In its most elementary form it appears as rhyme, word repetition and refrain; at its most sophisticated it achieves the intricacies found in the work of Dickinson and Hopkins. As readers and critics we may overlook its special contribution to meaning because the appeal of competing conventions is more attractive, because the melodic and echoic values are so overpowering, or merely because of the demands it places simultaneously upon the ear and the mind.

Ironically, though, it is the ear which is the easiest and most natural part of the critical apparatus to educate, as anyone who reads poetry to children will know. I believe that we fail to capitalize on the latent resources we all have for responding to patterns of sound (learned from infancy), and that once the significance of consonance as a meaning-laden, integral part of reading poetry is accepted, we can comfortably incorporate it into our ongoing, naturally developing response to verse.

3

If consonance provides a special form of coherence for the reader of verse, then it is possible, even probable, that the author 'intended' the effects it has produced. If so, then consonance may well play a major part in the composing process, whether it be used consciously, unconsciously or somewhere between the two (the most likely option). Certainly we are accustomed to assume that image patterns and elaborated metaphors are intentional and integral to the way poets construct meanings and explore experience. The modern habit of routinely scrutinizing the manuscripts and working papers of poets attests to our interest in the composing process for its own sake and for the implications such study holds for critical interpretation. I wish, then, to examine the manuscript of a short poem with a view to 'testing' our theory of coherence through consonance from the perspective of the writer composing. While any number of manuscripts might serve, I have chosen one of my own recent efforts because I know more about *some* of the decisions made during its evolution

Snowbound

Final Draft

Outside, the hedge-cedars
double under this weight-
less alabaster vise

Beyond, the roadway reverts
to river, bay, albino sea

In bleached degrees
the eaves succumb
to scroll and filigree,
incorrigible curves

Inch by hour
the porch is dwarfed
the house surrenders longitude
flattens toward sunset or dawn
dark or light it doesn't
matter when snows come
man-deep and more
than six-feet-by-four.

Stylized Drafts

3

(By the white degrees/*in bleached*/blanched *degrees*)
the (straight) eaves succumb
to scroll and filigree
(to shapelessness/*incorrigible curves*)

1-2

Outside, the hedge-cedars
(drift-*double*/tilt) under this weight-
less alabaster (squeeze/*vise*/frieze)

Beyond, the roadway reverts
to river, bay, (*albino*/chalk-white) sea

4

Inch by hour
(my fence/*the porch*) is dwarfed
the house surrenders longitude
(widens/*flattens*) toward sunset or dawn
(night or day/*dark or light*) it doesn't
matter when (the) snows (are/come/inflect/lay)
man-deep and more
than (six-feet-square/*six-feet-by-four*).

Though originally part of a series of poems on the same subject, this poem eventually came to stand on its own. The entire process of its growth from first scratching to 'published' form cannot, of course, ever be faithfully represented. In order to simplify the procedure, I have stylized the events without, I hope, distorting the original pattern of generation. By eliminating very minor changes in punctuation and lining, I have been able to display the stages of composition by 1) presenting the sequence of the stanzas as initially composed and numbering them for convenience, 2) placing in parentheses the options considered in order of their appearance, and 3) italicizing the final selection (not always the last alternative). What cannot be indicated is the actual sequence of all changes from draft to draft since this would entail laying out five or six (at least) 'complete' versions – an approach not available because I tend to 'work on' only one or two elaborated drafts with a busy red pen. Hence, I will indicate, as I proceed, the exact timing and progression of subsequent alterations as best as I can recall them.

The germination of the poem begins, as many do, with a rush of phrases *in medias res*. What eventually became the third stanza started out as the originating set of terms for the rest of the poem. The writer is in that purely heuristic state where words spin out almost automatically. In retrospect, I can see that I was reaching for some explication of the effects of a snowfall (one was raging outside as I wrote) in terms of increasing tension ("degrees", "succumb") and a shift in geometric configuration ("straight" – omitted early on – "scroll and filigree", "shapelessness"). A *necessary core* has been established; the germ of an idea and set of feelings have been achieved. What happens next? Here is where consonance begins to play its part in the *generative* procedures of composition. "White" does the job, it seems, but the power of "succumb" with its cutting *c* and muted *mb* influences (along with the extra assonance gained) the selection of "*blea*ched degr*ee*s", which also strengthens the notion of the progressive movement and whitening effects of the blizzard, as well as adding emotional overtones to the scene. But surely these '*meanings*' take precedence over the consonance? Not necessarily, for "succumb" is the key word so far in establishing that the events here will have dark connotations, that this kernel of a potential poem foreshadows something more than a pictorial narrative. Note too that "blanched" was tried and then replaced by the original option, as if the poet were testing out his own first, impressionistic responses. (We are talking here about seconds or minutes at most. Indeed it is the speed of first-draft composing that can never be adequately represented in manuscript analysis, yet is a crucial factor in our understanding of just how much trust poets place in their 'feel' for sound, rhythm and phrase-shaping.)

At this point, an idea, a nexus of feelings (powerlessness/ attraction) and a dramatic narrative have been realized as well as a concomitant set of related images and sound patterns (assonance of long *e*, consonance of *b* and *c/g*). But where does the plot move from here?

> (By white degrees/*in bleached*/blanched *degrees*)
> the (straight) eaves succumb
> to scroll and filigree
> (to shapelessness/*incorrigible curves*)

"Shapelessness" suggests that the play is over, that obliteration has been achieved. It's also a vague, hackneyed image as well as being only weakly related to the governing sounds (*p* and *s*). At this moment, "incorrigible curves" appears out of nowhere on the page, and the game is really on. First, the phrase itself is grammatically in apposition to "scroll and filigree", leaving the sentence more open-ended. Further, "*incorrigible* curves" deepens the ominous connotations hinted at in "succumb", and both adjective and noun are linked to the verb by consonance (the hard *c*, echoing as well the *g* of "degrees" and, in a more muted voice, the *v/s* of "ea*ves*" and its unvoiced cognate in the *f* of "*f*iligree" – a pattern to be picked up and modulated further on). Now the poet knows there is more to come. A propulsive and inevitable sequence of events has been set in motion with all the key poetic elements in place and a number of questions begging elaboration and resolution. How far will this accelerating/obliterating agent proceed? With what ultimate effects on the landscape and our feelings? In terms of the hypotheses we are testing, it is no more valid to say, within the context of the impetuous and dynamic first-draft phase of composing, that the poet initially generated and then selected (two different aspects of the process) among options purely on the basis of the semantic imperatives of the inchoate 'ideas' than it is to say that he worked from sound patterns, line structure, image clusters or dramatic development. All have obviously come into play more or less at once during the very early moments of genesis. In the case of "bleached" and "incorrigible curves", added *after* the originating core, I would speculate that both items had their passage from the well of the unconscious to the consciousness of the page prompted by the *generative* potential of "succumb", which harbours two of the consonantal motifs that will be seen to dominate the completed poem. Particularly in regard to the first-draft stage, it is fair to claim that the principle of consonance is both *an instrument for generating fresh alternatives and a structural feature for testing those alternatives* against already established consonantal and semantic paradigms. Indeed, this notion may help to explain what makes verse such a concentrated, multi-level, connotatively rich, and coherent form of expression. In the least we must admit that sound structure is an integral part of the construction of poems, coexistent and coeval with any other specialized aspects of poetic form. At best we might claim for it – on occasion – a central, even primary, role in the making of meaning.

More briefly now, let us follow the completion of "Snowbound" with an eye on both the generative and structuring potential of the consonance initiated by the kernel stanza above. Stanzas 2 and 3 quickly follow it, immediately numbered in the original manuscript as the first and second. The kernel stanza is then labelled number 3.

Outside, the hedge-cedars
(drift/*double*/tilt under this weight-
less alabaster (squeeze/*vise*/frieze)

Beyond, the roadway reverts
to river, bay (*albino*/chalk-white) sea

The poet knows he has completed act two or three, and begins the task of procuring the exposition. The snow, still unnamed, is placed more securely in the domestic setting predicted by "eaves". Its power, awesomeness, and paradoxically airy beauty are elaborated, as we might expect, in the imagery, but note as well that "he*dge*-c*edars*" is a complex modulation of "bl*eached*" and "c*u*rve*s*", and that "ala*b*aster" carries on the *b* of "*b*leached". All this is achieved without any further change. What about the options? There are three sets, each with three choices. In the first, "drift/double/tilt" appear in this order and almost simultaneously. "Tilt" continues the notion of angularity; "drift" has the *d* and *f*-patterns of the prior section but adds little to the geometric imagery; "double", though, suits both the developed consonance and the imagery, and even recalls the short *u* of "s*u*ccumb". In fact, seen from the perspective of the composing act, we have here examples of structural, consonantal linking like those we noted in the Dickinson poem. The poet in *his* mode is replicating the interpretive process executed later on by the reader. For both poet and reader (and the poet is *both* after his first draft), consonance draws words into association across the conventional rhetoric and syntax, and creates meaning not otherwise attainable. Thus "double" connotes not only a painful bending over but, in its necessary consonantal association with "succumb", it suggests something more helpless, sinister and inevitable. (Of course the reader of only the published version will see this in reverse order, but then poems are meant to be read many times so that initial responses are cumulatively cross-referenced and modified.)

Consonance, not unlike the syntax of the sentence, creates unique relations among parts, forcing, as syntax does, a fundamental configuration among words, which *then* permits us to comprehend the full import of their interrelated semantic meanings. As a hallmark of verse, consonance, strategically deployed by the poet, can act in much the same way that syntax does. The major difference seems to be that consonance deals only in the dimension of connotation whereas syntax maps out relatively fixed aspects of logical coherence that allows both the denotation and connotation of individual words to be activated more completely. Hence, the meanings inferred from consonantal linking and subsequent semantic association will be more tentative, open-ended, and subject to the constraints of other kinds of meaning in context. But these are the normal constraints we apply, with so much pleasure and controversy, to interpreting metaphor and connotatively ambivalent diction. None of this diminishes the validity of the notion that consonance appears to provide a unique form of making and getting meaning.

We see, for example, that sound values helped generate three options in the second set in the stanzas above. "squeeze/vise/frieze" are each related to "degrees", but "vise", on sober second thought, completes the metaphor implied in "double" (double-jawed vise?), loses the long *e* of degr*ee*s but fortuitously continues the minor motif begun with "ea*v*es", "*fi*ligree" and "cur*v*es". So "vise" remains. Here are a few more selected examples to illustrate the dual roles of consonance through the remainder of the poem.

Inch by hour

(my fence/*the porch* is dwarfed

the house surrenders longitude

(widens/*flattens*) toward sunset or dawn

(night or day/*dark or light*) it doesn't

matter when (the) snows (are/*come*/infect/lay)

man-deep and more

than (six-feet-square/*six-feet-by-four*).

On the structural, linking side, the *b*-pattern continues to develop associations among "succumb", "bleached" etc. and "al*b*ino", "*b*ay", "*p*orch", "man-dee*p*", "six-feet-*b*y-four" (carrying this latter phrase with its long *e* and part-rhyme – "four"/"hour" – back to "bleached degrees" and thus reinforcing the initial connotations of death in "bleached" and completing the geometric pattern suggested by "degrees"). Similarly, "come" (selected over three others) echoes "succumb" and thereby gains more meaning than such a pedestrian verb would normally attain. Other minor consonantal associations also accrue; for example, "po*rch*" with "*r*eve*r*ts", "*r*oadway", "*r*ive*r*" and "he*dg*e" (ch/dg are aural cognates), a significant linking because the verandah will suffer the same fate as these latter objects.

On the generative side, consonance tosses up for subsequent reflective consideration such options as "*ch*alk-white/al*b*ino", "*com*e/*re*f*le*c*t*" and "si*x*-f*ee*t-s*q*uare" (note in particular the modulation of "succumb" in "six")/"six-feet-by-four" (with its numerous consonantal references and its full and part rhyme). It is my contention that these represent the generative aspect of consonance simply because they are too complex (we have not looked at the modulations of *v/f* and several other minor patterns) ever to be self-consciously considered during their genesis, and yet most of them eventually yield extra-semantic meaning. Only when faced with alternatives (following their generation) does the poet bring his reflective powers into play, at which point his skills-as-reader take over much as ours do when we respond to the finished work. In the latter example *both* phrases are dripping with the accumulated, governing consonance; the final selection will be made after the fact and with a number of meaning-factors applied to the decision.

For a poet, and a reader fully sensitive to the ways in which poetry means, the meaning-potential of consonance is as natural and as unconscious as the basic grammar he uses to generate sentences; but that does not imply that he has little or no 'control' over its intentions and effects. We speak and write fluently only when the governing grammars *are* mostly unconscious – and make our reactions afterwards. As listeners and interpreters we are obliged to assume meaning wherever we can, until it fails to make sense. And the coherence of consonance is a very special part of the special methods of meaning intrinsic to poetry.

4

If mature poets and their readers use consonance as a way of realizing unique modes of meaning, is it possible that this sophisticated instrument is, like our native grammar, learned so early and so deeply that it becomes automatic and self-governing? One way of beginning to examine the question is to study the attempts at verse-making by children.[7] While a proper treatment of the subject would call for a separate paper (or more), some preliminary insights can be gained by looking at several representative samples.

The first represents the verse of a verbally gifted but untutored pupil (not uncommon in our schools). Kate, my daughter, wrote this poem at age fourteen-and-a-half. She was an engaged but not omnivorous reader of fiction (no poetry); to this point she had shown little interest in and no aptitude for imaginative writing of any kind; if she had encountered poetry at all in school, it was strictly incidental, pedagogically conventional, and coloured by stock response. This *maiden* effort was written, without major revision, at home, and eventually shown to me.

> I walk slowly –
> Sleet piercing my skin.
> I stop to ponder once again.
> My skin is raw,
> Though I feel no pain.
> Answers are few,
> Questions so plentiful
> Like the lone poplar
> In the forest of pines.
>
> I am the lone poplar.
> Unlike the people of pine
> I have no emotion.
> I will not sway
> In the wind of the pines' whispers.
> No longer do my leaves rustle
> For they've been crudely plucked,
> I stand bare and alone –
>
> To face the fast-approaching storm.
> The winds they blow no hope,
> They just lash at my bark,
> My only protection,
> I'll never turn my head
> To the malicious protected pines.

The incidence of consonance is marked and, in the absence of any formal rhyming (there are lots of part rhymes but they are, in our terms, merely a more subtle form of consonance), the major source of sound values. The predominant consonant, acting generatively and structurally as linking device, is the *p/b*-complement, signalled by "piercing" and reappearing in almost every line – in substantive verbs, nouns and adjectives – and culminating in the powerfully alliterative "protected pines", which also happens to be the controlling symbol. Similarly, the minor *c*-motif is announced in "skin" and carried through wonderfully associative images like "questions so plentiful", "crudely plucked", "lash at my bark" and again in "protected pines" where major and minor motifs merge. Here we see, in this naive but talented response to verse-making – with its sustained symbolism and driving, psychological undercurrents – all the best uses of sound: onomatopoeic, melodic, orchestral and generative/associative. And this from a girl who had read little poetry and heretofore composed none!

The next example is even more extraordinary, yet not untypical if my experiences in school workshops are any measure. Ken was a grade-eight student about thirteen years old. Like Kate he was untutored in verse (reading or writing), but unlike her he could barely write and was ranked by his teacher near the bottom of his class in English. In fact, the poems below were printed in shaky, oversize block capitals. A short film (*Legault's Place*, N.F.B.) and a tape of poetry being recited were used as stimuli for the exercise. No direct instruction was provided about what the 'poem' should look like, conform to, etc. After the tape and film were run, Ken and his classmates were asked to write a poem on the general subject of 'age', addressed by both tape and film, using the last seven or eight minutes left in the class period. Ken produced not only the three poems printed below but seven others just like them. He was writing as fast as he could manage and waving for more paper. Unquestionably, then, the results were first-draft, genuine, unstudied, uninstructed, powerfully felt compositions. The double stimuli and his own accumulated inner resources were all he had to draw on.

Dieing

Sitting hear
looking at the floor
Wasting time
Dying like a wounded animal
Nothing left
Dieing

Old

Old melting away
Old siting, doing nothing
old thinking
Old dieing

Clock

Ticking
Old Clock
Hanging
Doing nothing like me

Here, I believe, are the elemental components of verse composition at work (or play): construction by line or phrase-unit, feeling projected through image and metaphor, and consonance. Here is a boy who cannot in all probability write a prose sentence without a struggle and confusion, who does not know in the abstract what a verb and noun are, and yet he can turn the adjective "old" into a noun and fuse it with a participle to make a metaphoric expression like "old melting away", for which there is no ready or appropriate equivalent. How could he 'say' his feelings for the old man (observed in the film) in any more powerful a manner than he has? Somehow he has come to use the condensing/collapsing power of poetic language and syntax in a way that is both simple and profoundly complex. Moreover, all three poems are infused with the coherence of consonance. At the most basic level we find the use of repetition of the word "old" (syntactically transformed); more subtle is the *ing* of the verbals deployed throughout as a kind of inverted alliteration to help Ken find a structuring principle on which to shape his feelings. More subtle still is the *effect* of this *ing*-consonance when we realize that all of these verbals, associated by sound and syntax, are by definition *action*-words being used to describe the stasis, boredom and essential tragedy of a lonely old man and of aging in general. This 'action' is illusory and bitterly ironic, and Ken's repeated use of the device informs us that he has found a way for generating poem after poem until his feelings have been fully worked out. The third poem moves to a more projected metaphor or symbol in the "Old Clock" (seen in the film) and the putatively more sophisticated kind of consonance we earlier observed in the 'mature' verse of Dickinson: "ti*ck*in*g*...*c*loc*k*...han*g*...li*k*e".

Often we feel foolish in explicating children's poetry as if it were the product of mature germination and revision; yet more often than not we find that at its best it stands up well and glows even more brightly. It also shows us that our scholarly convictions about the naive and the sophisticated are less tenable than we supposed. Ken, unlike the mature poet (though he and Emily share a passion for continuous writing over revision), is not capable of reworking his first efforts in the same manner, of bringing his knowledge-as-reader to bear on the process. But at the first-draft stage of composing, the similarities are more significant than the differences. And one of the most salient of the former is the use of consonance as a generative and structuring instrument for making those kinds of meanings that lay at the heart of good poetry. From the reader's viewpoint, provided he is fully responsive to the effects of consonance and the constellation of devices in which it is embedded, there ought to be no significant distinction to be made between the best poems of the laureate and those of inspired beginners.

The coherence of consonance, like the speech we inherit and share, is a universal property to be exercised for the common good.

Local Culture and the National Will

One of the things that makes any discussion of local and national culture difficult is the elusiveness of the terms themselves, and in the face of such difficulty a tendency to simplify complex and evolving phenomena. As a writer of poems and novels who has spent some part of twenty-five years in exploring the extremes of the national and the local (Louis Riel and my own grandfathers, Nootka Sound and Point Edward), I have formed some opinions about each, about their nature and their value as culture. What follows is a sketch of these ideas, an argument if you like for the sort of book one rarely gets around to writing.

We begin by defining local culture, the root-flesh from which all subsequent culture is derived. Without it, nothing happens. In its radical form *local culture* (and by extension all culture) consists of those human products, communal states-of-mind and explicit and tacit communications whose principal purpose is to help establish an individual's place within the group. The group may be as small as a family or as large as a clan or a geographical region. What keeps it local and radical are these distinguishing features: the time and space, history and perspectives, legends and dialects that infuse the objects of culture – and whose general acceptance demarcates the existence of local culture – are *mutually shared* by members of the group. The amount of translation needed between the subject-matter or elementary form of the object and that understood by the "audience" will always be minimal. Theme will dominate variations, performance be valued over composition. This is the culture of tale, folk song, jig, communal quilt. Its well-springs are dream, collective memory, character, idiolect, love, existential terror. Its purposes are always clear-cut: the reinforcement of group and individual identity through coherence, bonding, and integration. Coherence through history – family, village, clan – actual and invented; bonding with the living members, the generations, the fantastic figures of legend; integration with these latter agents and with the exigencies of immediate space inhabited but not so easily mediated as time and history. Integration, of course, is the hope of both the group and the individual constituents. The need to belong – to be able to mediate between the existential objects we are born next to and the phantasma of our private-but-no-less-existential dream world – is particularly human and particularly hazardous. To surrender utterly to the phenomenal datum means the death of dream, to unleash the incoherent energies of dream signals the end of social harmony. Hence integration may be at times too strong a word; perhaps accommodation better fits as both individuals and the collective strive to balance the forces propelling them. In this sense the social group, so ubiquitous throughout human history, is both the reason for, and the necessary condition to, the formation of a culture and its effects. Until very recently, local culture and the regional social group were close to being synonymous. Each tribe of us, as it were, was more than a mere sum of its cultural objects and habits; our culture was a *process* with renewable by-products; it was as much the *impulse to create* demonstrative and binding signs, symbols, and rites as it was to conserve the manifest stories, iconography, and drama that resulted therefrom. Often the impulse was collective, emphasizing group values; occasionally it was individuated to remind the group that language is after all a colloquy of separate voices speaking from the common dark. Looking back, as we often do, at the surviving objects of an extinct tribe and attempting to reconstruct its culture is a risky enterprise for many reasons, not the least of which is the fact that sagas, sculptures, runes – once removed from the *living context* which they inhabited and hence robbed of their unspoken aboriginal magic, their capacity to incite and spawn tacit patterns of connectiveness – are dead objects whose resuscitation can only be achieved in a present-day, far-removed context entrammeled by its own cultural necessities.

While dynamic and elementary, local culture in order to survive must strike a balance between past and present, between conservation and necessary growth. It lives constantly with the danger of ossification if the forms become overly rigid, if time is not merely slowed but stopped, if variations are seen to threaten the theme. The result is what we might call *static local culture*, the source of much gratuitous criticism aimed at regional craft traditions or artificially revived enterprises like totem-pole reconstruction or the disinterment of folk song collections. The latter phenomenon, however, ought to be viewed with sympathy for it is probably symptomatic of a deeper malaise. Many of our regions in Canada are too new, too polyglot, or barren of any continuous traditions, and so they import – in desperation and holus-bolus – an intact regional culture from somewhere else on the planet. The most egregious example of what I call *ersatz local culture* is the adoption of country music from Nashville by large segments of the rural population, many of whom once had a thriving local music. They appear to feel more at home with a foreign regional culture than with the mass cosmopolitan culture being served up to them by their betters. While pathetic in a way, such behaviour does point up the powerful need for communities to feel they have adopted *their own kind* of culture *for their own purposes* – identity and bonding. It helps explain why a local balladeer in Woodstock, Ontario, can sing the praises of a hometown belle in flawless Tennessee twang. The long, arduous process of reintegrating and reinventing a genuine local tradition may indeed have begun. I find this sort of *aberrant local culture* painful but heartening.

There is, however, another variation of local culture which is perhaps the most significant one. Within thriving, genuine communities bound by cultural necessities, an artist rises from time to time who fashions individualistic works whose effects are too powerful, too true for the group to accommodate. Such an artist uses the very dialect, symbolism, and psychological geography of the place in order to speak (in part) directly to his group. Often he lives, creates, and remains in the community. I think of David Adams Richards or Greg Curnoe among many of our regional geniuses. Sometimes, however, the local community does not always fully appreciate the results, precisely because the perceived balance between individual and group identity has been tipped. The artists may go underground; sometimes they are adopted and lionized outside their region and move into exile or join a larger configuration of communities. But what has happened is irreversible: nurtured by the resident local culture or in opposition to its stasis, utilizing the mythology, iconography, and psychic history of the *locus*, an artist of extraordinary talent – a visionary with a command of craft who is driven to re-create the community through the imagination of one of its individuals – produces works of such power that they provide the basis for a new kind of culture itself: the transformational.

Transformational culture is often, even wilfully, confused with so-called "universal culture" and then set simplistically and deliberately against "local appeal" as if the two were antonyms in whose opposition lay some profound critical and anthropological insight. "Canadian writers will never be considered for the Nobel Prize until they start writing books about universal themes!" How often we have been compelled to listen to such nonsense in its various guises. When a work of transformational power is produced, it is grounded in the local, but that ground is thereby raised to the allegorical perspective. To the local "reader" the symbols will feel familiar but strange, their configurations novel and scary (I think of Winghamites coping with Alice Munro's stories or the valleyfolk puzzling over Buckler). Such works are addressed by the artist to himself and to anyone else who can translate, penetrate, and respond to the ideological surface. While instrumental music and abstract painting may "travel" more readily, literature, objective painting, folk song, and the plastic arts – where subject and formal elements are locally rooted – will travel only as far as their surface depictions, their referents, and the underlying *mythos* can be understood by any would-be responder (all three factors are operative, not just the so-called "universal types" somehow visible beneath the interfering clutter of the surface).

Furthermore, transformational culture is likely to be the result of an accidental but wondrous integration, in the mind of an individual artist, of his own local impulse with all his worldly experience. The transformational artist – far from hibernating in the local bush – soaks up foreign impulses of all kinds but always drives them downward and inward to himself and his own space and time – reformulating the local mythology in terms that 1) illuminate, for those constituents who can stand it, the locale in fresh, frightening, abiding ways, 2) allegorize both its substance and dialect, its surface and depths, its mores and neuroses, and 3) revalue it through the individual imagination and waft it abroad to any of those other communities or individuals "out there". Regionally transformed such knowledge is, but never fully universal; that is a contradiction in terms. Those outside the immediate culture (region, province, country, continent) can respond to it only as far as its particular paradigms can be understood. All culture travels and has in the process to be translated. For example, to put the case crudely, what remains of *Hamlet* when translated into Russian or read in the original by a grade-twelve student in Regina on a snowy Saturday? Quite a lot, we think, though not all and certainly not the same everywhere. Even though it is not universal, *Hamlet* does travel. Indeed its record of successful travelling is what is fascinating from the perspective of cultural analysis. There is no official translation for a work that transformed its own culture and still has the potential to transform the culture of communities not yet realized. Like all products of local culture that rise to the level of the transformational, it was prompted by local historical circumstances and is even now moving through historical time and subject to its ruthless emendation. Each community who adopts it – each individual who opens his mind to it – must effect a new translation, and unless some parody of cultural activity is in vogue, must integrate it with his own genuinely developed experience. The idolatry often associated with the response to "great" foreign works is always a perversion of culture, as is much of the literary criticism which attempts to fix such works "once and for all time".

One is still willing to make an effort to read (i.e., translate) Donne's *Songs and Sonnets* because the locus of its feelings and "statements" lies in relationships we can still understand and be deeply moved by. Nonetheless, to deny that the conceits, ornamentation, and political references are not partly impedimental is both untenable and perverse. Donne's literary conventions, dialect, and politics are not our own, in particular or in general. It appears that no one is willing to admit this obvious cultural, one might even say anthropological, fact, for fear perhaps that the great artists of the past will either be instantly debased or automatically devalued *vis-a-vis* that local and contemporary. That is patently absurd. Our response to art doesn't work that way. Many individuals, even communities, will be happy to respond to *Hamlet* despite the layers of translation necessary and even find it more rewarding than the latest Canadian melodrama downtown. The two kinds of response – to the foreign and the local – and the myriad variations in between are not mutually excluding. What one may be forgiven for thinking is that many teachers and cultural imperialists fear that if the illegitimately formulated mystique of the "great work" is allowed to deflate, their student/client responders will either reject the work out-of-hand or enter into a genuine, transformative and dangerous liaison with it.

If all genuine works of culture emanate through transformations from the local, what then can a *national culture* be? Given the size and multi-regional nature of most modern nation-states, it is not unfair to claim that there are few, if any, monolithic cultures at the level of the nation-as-a-whole. Certainly Canada fails to qualify on ethnic, linguistic, and geographical/historical grounds. However, if we define a genuine national culture as a multi-communal one, then we can see more clearly how local culture gets transformed to regional, provincial, and national configurations (not syntheses). In this latter view, a national culture would be characterized by the shared, non-threatening exchange of cultural experiences, values and artifacts – within a federated state like Canada – between the consenting member-groups. Ideally a set of affinitive local cultures would exchange cultural effects in order to allow the tension along the axis of individual/group or small-group/large group/foreign community to initiate positive responses, and to promote accommodation to, and integration of, new forms and new knowledge where risks are bearable and growth assured. In an ideal multi-communal culture, transformational artists would be encouraged to send their works abroad and in turn be open to influence from reciprocal artistic experiences. Here, too, the accidents of history and circumstances can be accepted and continually transformed into the vision of ourselves we need to survive.

Obviously Canada is not an exemplum of such a culture. Here, as in many other western nations, we are victims (or impresarios) of a *pseudo-national culture,* which in its virulent forms breaks down the will of local cultures through deliberate social policy or the mindless intervention of modern technological systems that leave the regional community mesmerized, exhausted, or happily drugged. It would require another paper longer than this one to elaborate the complex ways in which the modern nation-state has adopted and deployed technology to disrupt and destroy the luxuriance of local culture (not to mention the intimidation and outright annihilation of transformational artists everywhere). However, it may be sufficient here to point out that the main features of this technology (a true antonym for local culture) are these: (1) mass media and mass communication systems which allow bogus foreign culture to inundate the regions; (2) a consequent increase in the pace, volume, and repetition of alien "structures" (bogus or genuine) which induces anxiety, narcosis, or at best aberrant imitation; (3) an irresistible temptation to use these instruments to control, to propagandize, to purvey an "official" view of culture, or merely through neglect to allow a metropolitan culture (like Montreal or Toronto) to overwhelm. As we have noted, the growth of local culture and its transformation and dissemination require time, stability, trust, and the means to communicate its quiet news.

As a nation we have in Canada an ideal conglomeration of communities in which to foster a genuine national culture of the multi-communal type. So far we have remained relatively uninfected by the more totalitarian perversions of modern technology. We may ignore out own artists, but then we don't torture them either. We are a federated state and intractably regional. Nonetheless, technology as an instrumental system and as a way-of-thinking has arrived on these shores. Technology itself is inimical to the preservation of local culture. The effects of mass TV and radio – despite the well-meaning distortions of the CBC – are already apparent. The importation of ersatz foreign cultures is accelerating apace. Our national government is more and more seduced by the efficiencies of centralization; soon it may be hungry for a representative transcontinental pseudo-culture to peddle abroad. For the moment it seems content with province-bashing at the political level and at the cultural level – when it thinks of it at all – seems pleased with the collocation of frozen folk-cultures it piously labels "multi-cultural" – surely an unconscious parody of a multi-communal national culture wherein each of the regional groups (including of course ethnic communities) would have a living, developing *anima* of its own – fostering, tolerating, or flinging abroad transformational works to those mutually committed enclaves who, for these moments in time at least, have decided to try to become as capacious a community as their imaginations will allow.

Culture is both a transformational and a conserving phenomenon. Without it no community or nation long survives in any terms we would call human. Because it is local, psychological, and grounded in time, it cannot be manufactured. As a nation this country has been singularly blessed to be able to nurture local culture, encourage transformations within it, and absorb – if it is at all possible – the terrifying incursion of the technological into our lives. Some understanding of the imperatives of local culture and the shibboleths of cultural industrialism may help us in the critical years ahead. As a nation of federated communities we will also need more will and determination than we have shown thus far.

Old Photographs and the Documentary Imperative

When the editors of *Canadian Literature* asked if I would write an "impressionistic piece" about photographs-and-poetry (old photos, fresh poems) in response to some recently published collections of the former, my initial instinct was to reply in the negative. After all my own historic forays into family photography (Kodak-disc at the ready) have not exactly been prize-winning ventures. For years I left my autograph in the form of a thumbprint at the bottom-right corner of each snapshot; my human subjects invariably moved half-an-inch faster than the shutter speed could tolerate; I was, I am now certain, the fool that contemporary hi-tech cameras are being proofed against. Further, on the appreciation side – the response to design, shading, soft-focus, and the myriad other curlicues of the craft – I am apparently just as inept. Several former friends have hinted that I suffer from a sort of tone-deafness of the eye. They could be right.

Nonetheless I said yes. Even before I received the aforementioned books for 'review', or indeed even knew their titles. What had occurred to me, as I thought about the task, was that I had, not long ago, published a book of poems heavily encumbered by photographs (*God's Geography*, 1982). It would be assumed that the author had both an interest in, and some understanding of, just how photographs and poems could be made artistically harmonious. Moreover, I decided that enough time had elapsed since the compilation of *God's Geography* – between 1976 and 1979 – that I could, and should, return there and think about my own motives and procedures. So, I said yes; and while I waited for the books to arrive, I set about reflecting on the lengthy journey that had brought me through the creation of five volumes of poetry to the radical (for me) collage effects of *God's Geography*.

Photographs, of course, are artifacts. Photographs from our past – those lovingly spliced in family albums, artfully arranged in archival collections, or randomly encountered while leafing through old newspapers and magazines – are artifacts from the past. They are as substantive as the rusty plough in the county museum or the tea-set in the model kitchen of a pioneer village. But they don't tell the same kind of story. Like the print that stares yellowly out at us from a front-page news item accidentally uncovered at the bottom of Aunt Fanny's trousseau-trunk, old photographs are more than images of ancient objects and frozen gestures. Each of them, front-page or album photo, has a voice, waiting to be heard. We can glance at the photograph or skim the newsprint, and toss them aside with the same nostalgic sigh we might give to a great-grandmother's lace doily. We might engage in an orgy of free association, letting any of these artifacts-as-objects prompt in us that bittersweet meandering through the times and places of our personal memory. But if we *read* the news item, let its smothered voice unravel and catch hold, we enter into a remarkably different arrangement with our past and our own connection to it. We are allowing the artifact to speak *at us*, to retell, at least in part, its own story. We may add much to it; our memory and our associations do not disappear, but they are focussed in special ways. The news stories, headlines, and letters-to-the-editor that I selected for inclusion in my first book, *Riel: A Poem for Voices*, brought with them their own powerful, unalterable meanings. I merely took advantage of them, releasing them to new possibilities. What I had not realized back then (1968) was that old photographs had the same potential. I had been a closet collagist all along, despite the unauthorized labelling of my major work (*Riel, Coppermine, Borderlands,* and *Tecumseh*) as narrative. We are all, it seems, misunderstood.

In retrospect, it is clear that my use of excerpts retrieved from the archives of the period I was exploring was compulsive: hang-him-high letters to the *Globe* about Riel, selections from Samuel Hearne's own journal (subsequently deleted from the published version, but nonetheless vital to the way *Coppermine* got itself written), descriptions and accounts from the explorers of the Northwest Coast in *Borderlands*, and, among other contemporary items, excerpts from Tecumseh's own speeches faithfully recorded and translated for us by an earlier but no-less-paranoid version of the CIA. By the time I got around to writing about my own region and family in *A True History of Lambton County* (1977), I had exorcised an obsession with 'national' consciousness and larger-than-life protagonists and with the narrative mode of arrangement, but not it turned out with the use of print-document to be set alongside of or (a new tactic) integrated into individual poems. Indeed, the line between poem and document itself becomes blurred. One 'poem' – "The Lambton Gavotte" – is composed entirely of excerpts from local archival materials. So far though, 'document' is still limited to selections from print sources; no photographs yet.

But two things emerge as I review or re-see these artful and chance events. One: in whatever particular fashion I used a document from book to book, I was always concerned to let the item, at least initially, tell its own story. I did not think of a news feature, a letter, a journal entry, an advertisement, or a speech as a 'found poem' in any conventional sense. It was intended always to resonate – thematically, rhetorically, symbolically – with the invented narratives (my poems). None of this, I believe, was done very much at a conscious level (very little is).

But after scanning microfilm for three hours and having a passage from a newspaper 'jump out' at one, I realized that some part of my poet's instinct was invariably operating despite eyestrain and lumbago. Surely part of such a gestalt experience is that the story was making some point of its own, beyond its mere appropriateness as a counterpoint in the poem I was developing. Many such obvious links, to themes or events or symbols already established, appeared every half hour or so during my searching; and were routinely rejected. But I never failed to *know* when I would pull out a *bona fide* artifact and find some use for it in the evolving collage of the whole work. More often than not, a document so blessed resulted in a fresh poem or on occasion a shift in the direction of the book's overall story. Documents were so selected *during* the writing of all five of my so-called narrative collections, never *before* or *after* the 'real' poems had been conceived. While it is not for me to explicate the precise role or meanings of particular archival selections (I've faked it nicely on occasion), in general I feel now that several of the following aspects of such artifacts contributed to their existential power: appropriateness (as above and never the sole criterion of selection); density and closure (some cogent revelation expressed succinctly and somehow completed even though it usually was, in the original, part of a longer flow of thought); disclosure (where the form, rhetoric, or idiolect unwittingly revealed, from our/my perspective much more than the speaker wished to tell); and documentary typicality and authenticity.

This latter quality of the print excerpts I've used needs separate explanation, because it represents in effect the second major point about my obsession with them through the years. Not only must the documents be thematically appropriate and have an intrinsic story-of-their-own, they must also be typical and true – aspects that can, of course, be embedded in the other qualities. Put another way, an excerpt must *document* for me some *typical* point (motive, prejudice, rationalization, quirk of speech, quality of character) of the historical moment it simultaneously emerges from and keeps frozen for future use. For me, it had to be authentic, to have been written at the time I represented it to be when I utilized it in my own work. My role was to discover it, excise it from the obstreperous flow of its contemporary distractions, choose its voice, let it speak from its own free-standing dais and invite it to collide, as it wished, with the poems and other documents I set it amongst. Only rarely did I edit, and, I trust (no affidavits on this issue), in the first instance only to release the existential tale itself. That is I tried not to edit it to fit some immediate requirement of the larger work. (In *Riel*, I could not find an archival letter from one of the Canadian troops during the First Rebellion, despite a long search, and so regretfully resorted to inventing one, a manoeuvre not unnoticed by reviewers. Such exceptions prove the rule that governed my intentions during these years). Nor was I interested in realigning or otherwise tidying up the originals to make them look like found poems. Letters stayed letters, diaries remained diaries.

Why? What did it matter? How many readers would check the authenticity of a letter if the poetic uses of it were artistically pleasing? Especially in light of the fact that in the invented stories of my accompanying poems I appeared to have little qualm in altering actual events under the traditional dispensation called poetic licence? (For example, in *Riel*, Thomas Scott is represented as a blasphemous buffalo-hunter; he was blasphemous but no bison-killer.) No one seriously disputes an author's right to make his own artifacts out of history's. It's always been *caveat lector*. The answer to the question is simply that I still do not know why in reconstructing history-as-art I have such a passion not for the accuracy of historical interpretation or even for a strict fidelity to sequence and event, but rather for the authenticity and ontological status of any documents that I choose to incorporate in the wider artistic statement. Moreover, while my long poems (narrative, collages, who knows?) are freely interpretive and my indeed have more meaning as present-tense allegories than as 'readings' of history, I need to confess at last that whatever the purpose or result of my compositions, my methods and touchstones for validity were irredeemably documentary. For years I pursued historical figures relentlessly among the flotsam of our recorded history. I always preferred, even in the imagined sequences, to *base* the account on an actual one, or have it at least prompted by a fact from the archival remains (Tecumseh's having read *Hamlet* is mentioned in one of the contemporary chronicles, and though it's disputed by learned historians, I am comfortable in writing a poem from that 'fact' because it *was* documented, somebody believed it and wrote it down, and therefore it *is* authentic). In sum, both in my specific handling of actual documents and more generally in my treatment of the history itself, I had (and still have) an inexplicable reverence for document and historical event. And this, paradoxically, in face of the fact that I may not be in any common sense of the term an historical poet, a poet like Pratt, say, who writes documentary narratives. (A further paradox exists in my prose-fiction work where few of these constraints apply, and none with the same cogency of obligation,) Indeed, my book-length poem-collages are not documentaries. But they are imbued, in their method of composition and in their use of archival materials, with a documentary spirit, a belief that documents retrieved 'whole' from that part of the past which is still continuous with our genealogy and our dream-memory are to be treated with the respect we normally reserve for sacred texts. They are neither to be forgotten nor may they be deployed by subsequent generations as they would. They bind us all, like beliefs that both liberate and enslave.

So, at long last when I was prompted, for no reason known to reason, to expand yet again the range of documents in composing my first genuine collage-poem, *God's Geography*, I added the spoken word. Beside the poems I would place, as documents, excerpts from tape-recorded interviews with elder residents from the region under study – the village of Point Edward. I used the same criterion as for the printed material – 'scanning' hours of free-fall talk for two-minute gems, to be transcribed as faithfully as possible and intercalated. The newspaper excerpts were, for the first time, created as single-page collages of news items, where type-face and shape and arrangement were to be part of the constituent meaning (that is, each was a free-standing 'statement') as well as setting up associative resonance with the other documents and poems.

These other documents now included photographs. I set out to find old album-photos of past life in the village. More than half of the photographs in *God's Geography* are genuine archival documents; they selected themselves in ways no different in kind from those I had been implicitly using for over ten years to select print materials. What changed, with the taped excerpts and the photographs, was not my customary search for appropriate and authentic items but merely the shift in the formal elements native to the new media: quality of 'voice' in the recorded interviews and the pictorial power of the photographs (not their artistic strengths, of course, but their capacity to project complete and typical stories). I have some doubts that my ability to appreciate the art of photography has improved over the years (it may have), but no question remains as to why, after years of circumspection, I was able to discover *photographic* documents with the same enthusiasm and certainty of their appropriateness: I was brining to them not only the layman's love of old photos – with their capacity for memory-jogging, for inducing synesthetic side-trips of feeling and association – but the Canadian writer's long and mysterious passion for the documentary icon, whatever transformation it appears in.

To me, even now, our national obsession with document cannot be easily explained away as a childish grasp for the literal; a deep fear of the spiritual and the numinous; a clinging to the local, regional, and immediate; a century-long quest for some elusive identity; a beaverish sort of collective imagination; a resistance to the future itself. Any or all of these may be involved. But they are not sufficient. As writers as diverse as Findley and Atwood or Laurence and Kroetsch have shown us recently, we have already made much of our history and its legacy of document. And we are apt to make much more of them.

The books arrive, four of them. They are a banquet for those eyes the memory enlists for its daylight ramblings. I deploy the whole range of conventional responses in reading and savouring them. The two archival collections coincide with the historical periods I have just been writing about, 1880-1920. In *Canada: the Missing Years* and *An Atlantic Album* I find a rich lode of information, telling detail, association, and reverberation. Although each book is arranged by theme or topic, the effect is still one of the family photo-album. The delights are random; the surprises often unintentional; artful composition resides next to amateurish eagerness, and the former does not always win the day. I am invited to indulge in an idiosyncrasy: I look for the anomaly, the unsalient detail that runs cross-grain, and am rewarded. In a photograph of a visiting Chinese dignitary, with all eyes and all feet aimed worshipfully in one direction, a mongrel (uninvited by the booster cameraman) is loping the other way. "The Siwash Madonna" (there are many shots of Indians and Eskimos), a woman of great dignity, sports a raffish pipe clamped at a most unreligious angle between her teeth. In these two collections, as well as the two professional anthologies by individual photographers, I find pictures that exude a great beauty and power-of-feeling, some because of the conscious artistry (maybe I'm no longer a visual dyslexic: I even respond to the vegetable abstractions of *My Father's Garden*) and some without its assistance. In *Canada: the Missing Years* (p. 66) one photograph in particular haunts me. It is an 'artful' shot of a bride on her wedding day: alone, awash in sunshine, lace, foaming flowers, a pleasingly arranged play of light and nurturing shadow. As a deliberate statement it is both subtle and iconic. But even without such evident artifice the look upon the girl's face, the way her hand cradles the bridal bouquet, the absolute sense of repose and hopefulness she portrays to the viewer – all, we are certain, were there in her and her being before the lens composed its objects, and would remain long after its click.

It is this ability of human subjects to stare past the camera that is such a wonder: the capacity to look right at us out of the momentariness of their time, as if they knew we would be waiting for them, acknowledging as they must the hegemony of the camera, yet surrendering nothing to it except the superficial accoutrements of that time and circumstance, holding their being intact and simultaneously transmitting its essence to the unknown viewer, to the idea of the future itself. How can I feel such an aching sense of loss while at the same time experiencing a profound exhilaration – not only because this photograph as artifice has captured both the scene and the girl-in-it but because she has also somehow transcended it as art. By some sleight-of-hand, she has permitted the serene joy of her wedding day to be frozen-in-time while reminding us that its quality-of-being exists ontologically outside the graphic moment, and can still exist outside of time in the mind of the perceptive viewer. This beautiful young woman was there that day in all her beauty, the photograph assures me of it; but she herself is telling me more, inviting me to listen to the whole story, and to let that story live and thrive, both then and now. After many hours of browsing and staring, I return to half-a-dozen photographs, out of the many hundreds, that have this power to mesmerize and project something we can feel but not explain: the cover photo of *Canada: the Missing Years*; "The Taylor Family" (p. 52), "St. Michael's Orphanage" (p. 60) and "Una Gibson" (p. 130) in *An Atlantic Album*; "The Dandelion" in *The Mind's Eye*. These are the very kind of photographs I would retrieve for use in one of my longer, ongoing works. They live in their own right as document and icon. They are begging us to rediscover, to disclose, to use them one again not merely to re-remember but rather to begin preparing ourselves to be worthy of our future.

At the moment I happen not to be working on a sequence of poems. On the other hand...

References

– R.E. Balch, *A Mind's Eye*. Fredericton: Goose Lane Editions, 1985.
– William Eakin, *My Father's Garden*. Winnipeg: The Winnipeg Art Gallery, 1985.
– Don Gutteridge, *God's Geography*. Coldstream, Ont.: Brick Books, 1982.
– Patricia Pierce, ed., *Canada: the Missing Years: the Lost Images of Our Heritage, 1895-1924*. Toronto: Stoddart, 1985.
– Scott Robson and Shelagh Mackenzie, eds., *An Atlantic Album: Photographs of the Atlantic Provinces, Before 1920*. Halifax: Nimbus Publishing, 1985.

Appendices

Don Gutteridge's Mythic Tetralogy

by Keith Garebian

Three parts of Don Gutteridge's tetralogy appeared in the seventies, so there is no analysis of them in John Moss's *Patterns of Isolation*, Doug Jones's *Butterfly on Rock*, or Northrop Frye's *The Bush Garden*. Nor is there any particular comment in Frank Davey's *From There to Here*, Elizabeth Waterston's *Survey*, or *The Oxford Companion to Canadian History and Literature*. Gutteridge does get worked into Margaret Atwood's victimization thesis in *Survival*, but the insistent generalization, blatant oversimplifications, and flippant humour of that book would hardly tempt a critic to examine Gutteridge's poetry for something other than thesis fodder. Gutteridge's historical tetralogy — Riel (1968), Coppermine (1973), Borderlands (1975), and Tecumseh (1976) — is a relatively recent corpus, but right from Riel it is apparent to a perceptive critic that Gutteridge is more than a journeyman poet.

Superficially, Gutteridge appears to be a documentary poet along the lines drawn by Dorothy Livesay in a celebrated paper presented at York University, June 12, 1969. [1] His tetralogy — where each work can stand impressively by itself — does not follow the strict narrative pattern in Browning's or Tennyson's manner; nor does it place its chief emphasis on historical perspective — despite all its debts to such eminent sources as Samuel Hearne, Louis Riel, John Jewitt, and David Thompson. Unlike American epics such as Leaves Of Grass or The Bridge, Gutteridge's tetralogy docs not seem to create a single national myth, but reads very much like a group of long poems that are "based on topical data but held together by descriptive, lyrical, and didactic elements." Gutteridge's poems — especially Riel (subtitled "a poem for voices are meant to be read aloud; thus they join the ranks of other Canadian long documentary poems such as Marriott's The Wind Our Enemy, Birney's Trial of a City, Pratt's The Titanic, and Livesay's Call My People Home. The most recent preoccupations with the documentary form in Canadian poetry — Andrew Suknaski's Wood Mountain Poems, Michael Ondaatje's The Collected Works Of Billy

The Kid, Milton Acorn's The Island Means Minago try to be more than either simple reportage or skillful didacticism. They attempt mythmaking on a national scale, beginning with locale and extending, like Yeats's famous gloved hand, past the cobwebs of history to universal themes and myths. Always there is an insistence on symbolic significance beyond the mere themes or didactic force. Indeed, all the parts of the tetralogy tell real stories factually documented in fundamentals — for a myth's sake; and this myth is nothing if not that of a psycho-spatial man — doomed redeemer, freely adventuring explorer, or shocked captive-initiate.

Gutteridge, like Pratt, begins with historical data, but inevitably moves to create a poetic meaning for his stories. If we were to stand back from each of his four narratives, we would find four types of myth with their languages of symbolic translation. Riel, for instance, could be interpreted as a salvation-history, a story of a redeemer and his martyrdom. The symbolist Coppermine is in the old tradition of the quest. Borderlands is a myth of psychic integration and uses the motifs of captivity and cruelty. Finally, Tecumseh aligns with Riel in becoming an explicit myth of translation with Osirian analogies. In each case, there is an obsessive intensity of theme, but the entire form of mythos is clarified by Gutteridge's skillful deployment of language. The lyrical mode holds sway over all other styles, and diction and image show Gutteridge's preoccupation with transformations, with writing a language capable of expressing states of being.

Dramatized antithetical responses to land and life: the Métis response (personified and intensified by a neurotic Riel), and the white, colonial response. The first response is expressed through symbolism, lyrical and dramatic rhythm, while the second response is made explicit by flat prose.

At the beginning of this five act drama, we do not hear Riel's own voice, though we feel his spirit especially as this vibrates in the act of his walking with his father in Pembina in 1858. The Métis, we are told, find "in walking a togetherness of spirit," and the image of legs dominates the whole first section of Part One, particularly the first five lines, which use words like "walking," "steady stride," "lean-muscled," and "striding." The second sentence begins with a verb and (because of the omitted, but implied, connecting pronoun "they," i.e., Riel and his father) we have the emphasis on a verb that becomes the principle of continuity, the dynamic essence of the joining and separating imagery and the evocation of a linguistic characteristic of Cree (one of Riel's tongues) which can render a whole sentence or idea by a single word. A scholar has called the Cree language "one gigantic verb" because it often achieves through alterations in verbs what other languages achieve through declension or addition of nouns,[2] and the unmistakable impression we get from the third-person narrative opening is of one gigantic verb the act of walking in togetherness before space and event intervene and separate the two walkers.

The preponderance of prepositional phrases, two in almost every line, creates a density of detail and modification; and a concreteness derives from the several dozen nouns. As the fellow-feeling between father and son is built up, it becomes increasingly clear that Gutteridge is aiming for a tribal sense in the rhythm, imagery, and event :

> They were walking: as a Métis always walked
> Because a man could feel the Mother Earth through the palms
> Of his feet, and know the firmness of her flesh
> And the great unturning heart at the centre of her,
> Were walking because walking told in every stride
> Of man's moving over the earth in a passing as brief
> As a footprint, and because a Métis found
> In walking a togetherness of spirit,
> Of flesh knowing the same earth at the same turning
> Of the sun or the season, and a man moving
> Was like the wind's loving of the deep grasses,
> And did not stand like the rocks and die with stillness
> In the bones, and because walking made spring
> Out of muscle and limb, and a man could feel
> His body lean as a willow in its long greenness,
> And because there was joy in a Métis walking

With himself or his brother. These things had been told to him by his elders, and he had felt them.

Gutteridge's technical virtuosity is impressive. There is a taut quality in the buffalo hunt episode; a dream quality during the homeward journey, with slowly stretching syllables languorously and softly pronounced; a surrealistic overlapping of Thomas Scott's hysterical, sadistic laughter with the thundering noise of the stampeding buffalo; complex modifiers and descriptions from nature that (like the Cree tongue) are expressive and dramatically rhythmic in their rich vowel sounds, strongly aspirated consonants, verbal insistence, and varied tempo. Gutteridge is a prime synecdochist, for he takes the half wagon-half man configuration of the nomadic Bois-Brulés, and makes the wheel and circle emerge as dominant images during great colourful moments such as the gathering at Pembina.

But Gutteridge retains control over his language and his subject. Immediately following the opening section on the fellowship of walking, there is a prose letter by Charles Mair to The Globe in which the possession of land is made a bourgeois theme. An irony is obtained from the sharp contrast between young Riel's appreciation of the "great unturning heart" at the centre of Mother Earth and Mair's utilitarian approach to the question of prairie settlement:

But who should come in and possess this land? The question is easily answered. Any farmer who has $300 of capital and provisions to subsist his family for at least one year. He should also bring his seed-grain, a Pittsburgh plough, harrow teeth and a separate mower. And he would have no difficulty in selecting a farm. There is no Stobson's choice about it, 'this or none.' The cake is 700 miles long and 400 miles wide — and plenty of elbow room. Here at the western terminus of the proposed route from Canada are the three prime desiderata of the husbandman: land, wood and water. Land upon whose bosom has withered the enriching and procreant vegetation of centuries — land which drops fatness, as if in the fulfillment of prophecy: at once generous and abundant, and more durable than its tiller.

Mair, in an extremely ironic way because he is a poet writing so mundanely, suggests that he himself is much of a bourgeois materialist, seeking to convert raw land into productive landscape.

The rift between man and land, western landscape and colonial encroachment, is further dramatized by the image of the railroad. Here geometry and language are the twin nuances of meaning, for the railroad is a "straight line" to "horizon's roundness" and its "steel tongue" intones "its single word into empty western-sky." From the beginning, then, of European expansion farther west, there is a drama and difference in viewpoint and language. Where the Métis, because they are native to the prairie, commune with the dusty plains and the ghostly winds and lights of the aurora borealis (chepuyuk), the white colonizers impose their shapes on the land via their technology, and show off "brick towers," "stone spires," and "square roads." The names of concrete objects contrast with images of hands, feet, and heart, sometimes allied to and consecrated by Métis religious connotations: "he was happy just to feel his father's strides / Coincide with his own", "liking the feel of current pulling at his feet"; "twin-spires of the love / He learned at the altar of his mother's voice and arms / And hands." The community of feeling is intensified via the brief family-history of the Lagimodiöres and the repetition of the joining and separating images of feet, hands, and waters.

Though Gutteridge keeps his eye on event and connection, his dramatic evocations of personality and motive are strong. He shapes mundane, detailed portraits of such figures as Schultz, Scott, and Sir John A., which contrast vividly with an impressionistic, abstract rendering of Riel. Schultz, the western archetype of a political physician, is sketched as a staunchly respectable bourgeois, a freemason with Orange sympathies, bureaucratic, scheming, dyspeptic, arrogant, hostile to Catholics and Métis, and the prairie landscape. When he is first introduced to us, we take note of the strong patterns in his rhetoric. There are several adverbial phrases and clauses of concession that serve to make Schultz seem an archly sly conciliator who balances limitation against achievement, handicap against advantage.

Sir John A. comes off no less ironically, He is placed in a concrete world of objects, textures, and material values, and it is altogether a comfortable, elitist setting with its sideboard of American mahogany, its French port, crystal, scraps of parchment, quill, desk, stuffed chair, cigar-box, cut-glass decanter. With all the accoutrements of material comfort, Sir John A. entertains his distaste for the Catholics, and seems intolerant of anyone else. His character and Schultz's show that the new Northwest was to be an extension of Protestant Ontario. In the archetypal mode of a nation-builder, he is represented as an architect toying with building blocks of the country's future as his alcoholism weaves its dark river in his blood.

In contrast with his white antagonists, Riel is represented through emotion-charged symbols. Many key periods of his life are suggested — his "miracle" in 1874, his wooing of Evelina, his madness, exile, and trial — but, in general, there is little attempt at a direct revelation of character and certainly no explicit conjuration of what Kinsey Howard calls his "paranoid schizophrenia": wherein he was prone to grandiose illusions, egotistical spells of morbid introspection, mental excitability, a sense of persecution, and a conviction of divine mission. This is not to suggest that these traits or symptoms are not present in the poem.

Gutteridge does not take license with history; he merely departs from it in order to create something quite different.

If (as A. R. M. Lower argues) there is a point when history becomes myth, then Gutteridge's Riel is less a historical figure than a mythic one. He is not a rebel or insurrectionist but a line of resistance, a core of anarchic defiance. Yet Riel is not simply a symbol. If he were only this, then Gutteridge would have ironically repeated a historical mistake which once caused Riel to cease existing as a credible man. Though he is dramatized in opposition to Scott, Schultz, and Sir John A., Riel is an eloquent mystic, but here again irony prevails; for unlike the mysticism of orthodox Catholics, Riel's mysticism contains little or no joy. Instead, Riel's mysticism is based on certain magical superstitions, and expresses the transports of one who has not been estranged from his "primitive," native self. It is the root and delimitation of his messianic obsession, and leads to dreams and visions that are lyrically intense and totally alien to the minds and hearts of the colonizers.

There is another problem with Riel's characterization, and this probably arises out of the lyrical compression in the verse. To begin with, we do not have enough of the priestly rhetoric that often drenches the historical Riel's letters and sermons. And because of this deficiency, we do not obtain an effective contrast between the religious musings of a man obsessed with his self and the political writings of the same person where there is scant attention paid to personal fate. Nor is there enough ambiguity surrounding Riel's sanity. In Gutteridge's poem, we feel some of the soul-magnifying and mind-splitting force of his sense of destiny, but there is no sense of bizarre, anthropomorphic eccentricity, no grotesque distortions of the ego and religious belief that could possibly arouse solid doubts about his mental equilibrium. He is very realistically a David, awaiting the moment of his victory over Goliath: "David: fondling a / smooth stone, fingers seeking / The spring of its power." He is also very credibly a historical Messiah-manqué, "Moses confronted by a burning bush / That made the sky around it only blacker," and even, spiritually, a Christ among men. But he is not a madman, even in passing flights of uncontrol. His flashes of apocalyptic imagery (such as allusions to moving mountains, the Four Horsemen of the Apocalypse, and the Second Coming) make him an intense mystic, but they do not suggest he is hallucinating like one who has lost all distinction between the actual and the imagined.

The Ending of Riel Renders the poem apocalyptic in its symbolism and meaning, and this revelatory impulse links it to Coppermine, which, however, expresses a very different myth in a different style. The period of Coppermine occurs roughly a century before Riel's story, and now we are in the North rather than in the West. If Riel can be seen as a would-be Messiah's quest for his people's salvation, Coppermine can be interpreted as a Canadian version of the El Dorado myth.

Though Matonabbee, Chief of the Northern Indians, is the most striking character in this poem, it is the figure of Samuel Hearne who projects (through Gutteridge's poetic refractions) the white man's quest for the golden (read copper) one:

Matonabbee speaking

'Where the mouth of the grand river opens
To swallow
the sea, lies the Copper-mine:
And they say the metal sits there in chunks
As big as a bison's flank, and that once
When the dogs long ago dwelt there, they built
Giant fires out of the burning Aurora
And ate the copper flesh to make their
Blood hard, and what you now see there are bones
The gods have left behind in the daylong
Darkness, with only the Boreal light
Flickering on their nakedness like pale
Shadows of flaxne from some far-off dying
Hearth-fire of the Manitou.'

As Matonabbee tells this legend of the Coppermine, he seems to be enjoying the myth possibly because he gauges its special enchantment for Samuel Hearne and company. And the copper symbol is portentous from the start sinisterly so, for it is present in "gold visions" rejected by Midas whose gold-lust would normally not exclude anything golden.

Gutteridge projects through Matonabbee the sort of terror sprung out of the land and described by Frye in the Literary History of Canada. "It is not a terror of the dangers or discomforts or even the mysteries of nature, but a terror of the soul at something that these things manifest." In Coppermine the terror is temporarily attenuated as the Copper Woman myth enlarges. Geography is internalized and reprojected in lines that describe this mythic creature:

> Because she was a magic god-woman —
> Brown, like us, only her skin glowed as if
> Tiny fires burned in her flesh and shone through
> So you could see the rivers and runlets
> Her blood made, her whole body like a map
> With its own lakes and streams, and dark patches
> Where the land lay, and she had no deerskins
> On her, though the cold made the tent-poles snap, And snow
> melted on the flesh of her breasts, Buttocks and unlit cave of
>
> her thighs.
> They followed her over the treeless Barrens
> Through the darkness of night and day, their eyes
> On the north, which was the darkest part of
> The sky, and on the crevasse of those deep Woman-
> thighs, till they came to the place of The copper, and
> found her vision was true.

Everything is transmuted surreally into copper. Even the sexual sadism (just as strong in Borderlands and Tecumseh) is converted into something like a picture by Salvador Dali whose surface exoticism or polished strangeness does not obscure the psychological portent. The purpose of the surreal is not simply to excite the senses with a flow of apparently discrete images and colours, but to create a field of association that could develop into an integration of meaning. Though at first the surreal seems only unlikely or purely imaginative, its symbolism has an important psychic import. The surreal allows the poet the opportunity to indulge his artistic imagery, dispense with linear narrative, and — provided his synecdoche is clear enough — to build up a special significance for his motifs.

The method of Coppermine is largely symbolic and abstract — unlike that of Riel where meanings and symbols are connected through events that can be verified historically. Not that Coppermine is not based on history, but its composition appears to rely less on documented experiences though its depiction of the Eskimo slaughter is thoroughly accurate — and more on Gutteridge's power of lyric projection. Because the poet is interested in determining "what the eyes / won't tell," "what kind of mind" feeds on certain legends, he uses history as a point of departure or, at least, a core of radiation. The core is, of course, Hearne's obsession with discovering the source of copper, and the separate rays are the moments (scenes) of energy where the characters and the poet think "copper.' ‚There are accordingly periods of powerfully evocative symbols, moments when the struggle of the inarticulate seems to be overwhelming, phases of unresolved enigma, but the total work ultimately creates a significant story that, in using the archetypal quest form, finds analogues of being and types of knowledge that radiate from Hearne's adventure of exploration and discovery.

Gutteridge's external and internal worlds converge in Coppermine, and the mouth image becomes the chief expression of this phenomenon. Even in his fantasies, Hearne imagines himself being swallowed by the mouth of the mine, and his brain, the seat of reason and animal spirits, becomes metaphorically contracted to the mouth as space, light, and knowledge enter it.

This particular metaphorical alliance is especially significant, for it is an important detail in Gutteridge's synecdoche of psychic integration. Even space is represented as a "polar mouth / mind eaten / with its own appetite" and then, even more explicitly (but repetitively), its "magnetized teeth / nibble my brains / like copper meat."

The poetic voice of Hearne the explorer develops the drama of quest wherein the spirit seeks unity in the material world. In this regard, the geometric images (especially those of circles) are particularly effective- The first circle is, perhaps, the explorer's own eye, which besides throwing its focus on the sun (a cosmic eye) and the lines of vision measured by the quadrant (Hearne's third eye) , also looks at itself in a sort of Plotinian reflexiveness. For Plotinus, the eye would not be able to see the sun if the eye itself were not the sun. Hence we have traditional representations of the sun as an eye, or of Osiris and Christian God as a divine eye.

With his quadrant, Hearne acquires a third eye which is of dual significance. On the positive side, it symbolizes superhuman or divine awareness — much in the manner of Shiva's powerful third eye. However, on the negative side, a third eye is useless and is cast in darkness. In symbolist theory, the multiplicity is a sign of inferiority or psychic decomposition. It is the negative aspect which is stressed rather comically when Hearne breaks the quadrant:

> That day on my first journey
> when I broke my quadrant; they
> found it funny to see a blind
> man with three eyes.

The broken quadrant itself has an interesting significance, for the symbolism of quaternity implies the idea of a perfect order, the idea of the four natural elements that compose the universe in ancient Greek philosophy. Elsewhere in the poem, there is a moment imagined by Hearne when the square is circled: "Circles in a / squared eye: / earth affired. . . ." Here the squaring of the circle (or the circling of the square the order is reversible) is a geometric metaphor for stability, order, and materialized energy.

The point of Hearne's quest in this poem is not simply a geographical adventure or a colonial enterprise. It is abstracted into a quest for self-transformation. Matonabbee indicates as much by his own self-translation, when in dance he becomes a man recovering his sense of the eternal:

> Matonabbee as leader of the band
> conducts the supplicantatory
> dance,
> and for an encore swallows whole
> (like a slithering adder) a ten-inch
> rancid penis,
> then, puffed as a bullfinch struts and
> prances till we almost believe those
> antlers sprouting from his skull!

The energetic verbs and participles ("puffed, struts, prances, sprouting") align with the slithering adder and penis to signify both an inner spiritual and an external material strength — potential for the propagation of cosmic forces. The rising force is developed in the swelling dance where the verse follows the ascent of Matonabbee's force, moving upward from the sexual organ to the skull or realm of thought, at which point Matonabbee becomes a horned god or motif of eternity.

Samuel Hearne, however, never attains this height of self-transformation, though he experiences intensely an implosion of energy and consciousness: "the caves in the / brain flame inward / like igloos of / transfused light." Hearne is always uncertain of his direction:

> I am here, I know, was there,
> and there but
> if I lose this book map page
> where have I been?
> where do I go?

Despite his confusion, Hearne experiences an upward movement. This is catalyzed by Matonabbee's ritualistic dances, priogenitive prophecies, and symbolic references. It is Matonabbee who suggests the unity in multiplicity, although Hearne does not confine his images and symbols to Indian myth. He conjures up psychic significances from the Bible and Egyptian myth, and just as he sees in Matonabbee's slithering adder dance a spiritual ascent, he also intimates through his reference to Osiris rising, an evolving ascent; the very name Osiris means "he who is at the top of the steps."

Matonabbee, nevertheless, becomes the prime reference for Hearne as Gutteridge carefully represents the chief as a symbol of supreme spiritualization. There is a section, for instance, where Hearne observes, at first hand, the strange art of the medicine man-cum-conjurer:

> See Matonabbee the conjurer swallow a
> four-foot sword with his two-inch
> tongue! No tricks here no sleight-of-
> hand, naked as a bird he's plucked from
> tuft to toe!
>
> Old man in his death-throes waits for
> the magic to come: I watch his face, see
> death growing there like a masque of
> plaster bone, eyes adazzle with the

glitter of dying: last radiance of
mysteries not known magic
unredeemed.

But see how the conjurer plunges the
healing wand into his living throat, four
feet down to the blood and bone to the
heart of the mystery, see him pull the
cord to draw the magic out: glittering
sword adazzle in the darkness, bloody
tongue of radiance.

The sword has obvious magic power linked as it is to steel and hence to transcendent toughness or an all-conquering spirit. It is a symbol of spiritual evolution and in the context above, its association with light and fire ("glittering," "adazzle," "radiance") intensifies the spiritualization.

The "old man" is not a decoration or self-evident symbol. Besides being obviously a personification of age-old wisdom, he is the symbol of what Jung calls the "mana" personality — that is, the spirituality of personality caused when consciousness is over-burdened with matter from the unconscious death, in this context. [4]

It is Matonabbee who activates the magic of the sword, who releases the magic spirit welcomed by the old man awaiting death, and who, an hour later, takes on the crooked grin of a slightly ruffed bird, another symbol of spiritualization, as the old man is returned to life.

For all their strange beauty, a beauty coupled often with the obscene cruelty of violence, their intensity of imagery, their technical skill, Gutteridge's poems move inevitably towards the theme of death. Riel ends with the eponymous figure's abrupt hanging, with the cold "gray towers" of Ottawa dominating the fadeout. Coppermine charts its quest pattern surrealistically, but moves to the subject of a material death. Yet, this time the end is dualistic, for while Hearne begins his "long walk," he moves "back," i.e., returns his spirit to its cosmic source.

Borderlands, the next poem in the tetralogy, does not suggest a positive aspect to the death theme, for it shows John Jewitt, its protagonist-initiate, preparing for death without any spiritual translation. Borderlands, however, continues to show Gutteridge's variations on patterns. Unlike Riel, it is not about an ambivalent historical figure. Unlike Coppermine, it is not abstract in its method; nor is it a quest narrative. It is what could be called a story of initiation,[5] where the chief narrator is primarily concerned with self-preservation. The difference between quest literature and initiation literature is that between free exploration and captivity, or between ultimate purpose and a sense of immediacy.

Ostensibly based on Jewitt's account of life among the Nootka, Borderlands substantiates Frye's claim that "literature is conscious mythology" where its mythical stories "become habits of metaphorical thought."[6] This symbolic aspect crystallizes early as Maquina, the Nootka chief, articulates the perimeter of his geographical knowledge:

> Looking out is West where Ocean
> begins
> Looking in is East where Forest has
> his root
> We have no North: sun is
> always South of this coast
> North of here is nothing,
> nothing I want to know.

The primeval setting is radically different from the prairie in Riel and the surreal locale in Coppermine. Here myth grows out of "immense ranges of mountains or impenetrable forests" and "the pain of constant / distance" in the ocean. It is the myth of the captive-artisan, the blacksmith who is almost broken on the forge of his experience in an alien world. Jewitt, whose blacksmith-father wanted to be "Christ's armourer," discovers that his craft has dual significance: it is both his salvation and his weakness, for it permits him Maquina's favours but also keeps him the chief's captive. Maquina intends to be the strong hammer that strikes the metal of white man's flesh.

Here, as in Riel, Gutteridge develops a dialectic out of two contrasted ways of life, each apparently extravagant to the other. Where Mozino's Journal refers to a "barbarous sacrifice," Captain Gray and his crew take sadistic delight in murdering and committing outrages on the Indians: "we giggled as the / little puddings of their / brains dribbled out, / we took turns pissing / on their last smiles." The two tribes, Nootka and European, are closer in their instincts than they realize, for there is no difference between Maquina's lyrical description of the slaughter of the crew and Captain Gray's sadism except one: Maquina is coldly detached while Gray is emotionally and psychologically involved.

In other aspects, too, Nootka and European resemble one another closely. Maquina is ruthless in sex and war: he hacks his wife to death just as brutally as he assaults the Boston's crew. Jewitt, by the same token, becomes pure animal in his lust, and though some whites have objected that his idiom is too modern for the setting, we should remember that animal nature lies under the accretions of time and culture.

The shared savage instincts are set apart by contrasted languages which attest to distinctions in background, sensibility, and objective. Maquina asserts that the white man's way of fixing and cataloguing reality by rigid, unchanging names contrasts with the aboriginal proclivity towards multiplicity:

> My daughter has had three names and many
> more to come, when I have reached my last
> name on earth I shall already be dead, when
> my tribe runs out of words this coast will be
> blowing sand.

Maquina calls the white man's words hard, many-edged, angular, and sharp, but destructive. The irony is that while the white characters often struggle to give names to feelings and experiences, Maquina is an eloquent primitive. There is a strong clipped quality to Jewitt's diction, as though speech were being wrenched out of him.

The only time Jewitt becomes lyrical is when he describes his smith's craft. Here Jewitt is released from the burden of his coarse, ungraceful aspects and exults in the grace of his craft. Maquina, by contrast, consistently sounds a raw music that attests to the tactility of his being, a drum on which the universe sounds itself.

This eloquence is a crafty device which does not simply serve Gutteridge's lyrical impulse; it is a valid, psychologically correct product of passion and a human nature attuned to its setting.

Gutteridge, perhaps anticipating critical queries or objections, quotes Mozino's view on native eloquence and rhetoric:

Since eloquence has always been considered the child of vivid passions, and since these are capable of firing even the imagination of these savages, it should not seem strange that I affirm its existence among these islanders, and in passing forestall those critics who are quick to claim that the speeches placed in the mouths of these savages by certain writers are false, as if in order to speak with enthusiasm, making use of the most moving figures of speech, it is necessary to attend universities, to read books entitled 'Rhetoric,' and be ridiculous mimics of Marcus Tullius. To be eloquent, it is enough to follow freely the impulse of nature, whose mastery created the most celebrated orators of Greece.

What Borderlands amounts to, then, is a literary documentary where the desire to impress by a cumulative piling of effects diminishes its intrinsic dichotomous nature. At once direct, immediate, colourful, and powerful, Borderlands does not move deeply enough into realms of the archetype. We see that Maquina intuits the symbolism of salmon as the fish of wisdom; we know that the Bear ceremony has a significance beyond the merely sensational enigma impressed upon Jewitt; but the symbols do not amount to much in the general scheme of the poem. What we tend to remember best are the sexual sadism, certain exotic ceremonies, documented in Jewitt's original journal, and Maquina, who despite an impressive theatricality, integrity, and strength, does not overwhelm Jewitt.

The fundamental problem might be in Gutteridge's tendency to oversimplify the captivity story. His poem misses the motive for the chief's slaughter of the crew; it also misses the striking indignity suffered by Maquina, following Captain Salter's reproach. The poem fails to become the tragedy it could have been, and becomes a melodramatic narrative where Jewitt prepares for death and Maquina reasserts his "sea-dream" mortality.

The final part of Gutteridge's tetralogy returns us to Cosmos and epiphanic translation after exploring the borderland between history and myth. Tecumseh is, like Riel, an example of conscious mythologizing, and like Riel, extends from historical circumscription to a psychic internalization of the land and its various impulses.

The first part of Tecumseh provides us with pioneer dreams in French Quebec. There are various dreams projected in this section, that of a seigneur who is full of alcohol, blood lust, sex, and tawdry religiosity; one by a young woman and her mother, for both of whom reality is paradoxically an illusion of security and permanence; and two dreams by pioneer father and son who struggle to make the land fit their dreams of colonization and prosperity. These dreams are counter-pointed by Tecumseh's in Part Two, where the Indian strives to find a language appropriate and powerful enough to free the figures of dream: "my tribe's history / the necessary nightmare." There are several other elements as well, interludes, commentaries, historical expositions, meditations, a proclamation by General A. P. Hull, letters, and orations, but the predominance of dream renders this poem apocalyptic, and when we view it in the total context of the tetralogy, we see how the apocalyptic is a frame around Gutteridge's mythic mode.

As in all major works of prose and poetry about colonial Canada, it is the white man's dream of imposing himself upon the land that degenerates into a horrible nightmare wherein the external is internalized. Just as with Margaret Atwood's pioneer, who grows progressively insane as the land invades his resisting mind, the Quebec habitants are imprisoned in "cages" of their own making and become victims to their own paranoid delusions of security and permanence.

The colonial dream of civilization is protected assiduously by the various emigrants, but no dream remains inviolate:

> The dream of civilization I carried
> with me over the borderless ocean
> kept pure in the stink and rabble of
> the ship, have guarded here against
> all enemies — needs room to
> breathe, as well, will soon be feeding
> on itself.

No matter how zealously the bishop attempts to assert pioneer endevour and instruments of colonization, his apology is a weak resistance to the inevitable power of the land which compels the pioneers to admit that their log-walls are only an illusion of a home, "a domestic fiction" which ineluctably becomes a squelched dream.

Pioneer effort becomes grotesquely obsessive, but even the most grotesque human aspiration cannot match nature's grotesqueries. Father and son, both full of harsh labour, cannot force the land into a Procrustean adaptation to their ambitions:

> But the big trees remain beyond
> the clearing beyond the arc of
> hand or axe, nightmare or dream:
> in the coldest day they etch their
> grotesquerie across the whitest
> sky.

In the end, the son wants freedom from both his father and the land, the father is swallowed by his own dream, and there is an overwhelming sense of defeat despite the advent of nationalism and territorial protectionism.

Tecumseh's dream is to reclaim the land his people have surrendered to the white man. What justifies this dream is not simply a moral right of re-appropriation, but a fundamental understanding of nature that is resisted by the white colonizers to whom land is simply property or a possession that is without luminousness.

As in Riel, the political element is strong, particularly with the genocidal charge laid against the Canadians, and the subtle American strategy of exploiting Tecumseh as an agent for their own imperial expansionism. But the controlling dialectic (as in Riel and Borderlands) is expressed by a clash of symbols and values in the white colonial language of steel (the railroad a "steel tongue intoning / Its single word into empty western sky") and the Métis language of spiritual brotherhood. In Borderlands this clash is polarized in two modes of language, the rigid tongue-sounds of the whites and the perennially recreated language of the Nootka's never-depleted supply of words. Now in Tecumseh we have language that suggests a primeval myth, and the images (as in Scott's Laurentian poems and many sections of Pratt's Towards the Last Spike) spring out of the elemental landscape, of rock older than first bone, "seamed with myth / with hieroglyphic runnings / sealed by a silence / that stilled / the first and vital Word." We have the aggressive, destructive language of the western colonizer whose speech, like his pioneer activity, testifies to a ruined dream feeding on itself, and is expressed with energy but without love or understanding.

And we have the second language, the self-conscious, visionary utterances of Tecumseh, chief of the Shawnee, who tries to unite different tribes against the U.S. and save them from extinction.

Gutteridge generally finds the right sensuous lyric form to vitalize his narrative and absorb the prosaic ironies of miscellaneous documentation. His diction is powerful but beautifully simple except when he tries to express a character's intuitive intelligence by means of sophisticated abstraction. At these points, Gutteridge's imagery becomes obtrusive and anachronistic, especially when it issues from Tecumseh in moments of intense lyric self-consciousness. With Tecumseh, Gutteridge too often strains western diction into expressing an acute anguish and sensitivity whose pain is older than language.

But there is achievement even in this failure, for Tecumseh is an impressive drama of translation. Despite his mutilated corpse, Tecumseh remains the unstilled voice of conscience in a land that has the scattered pieces of his body. His Osirian dismemberment is a deliberate mythic reference, and when his resurrected spirit is said to enter all things and speak to us in a way that "humiliates the air" and breaks the chronology of his people's despair, we know explicitly that Gutteridge is exploring the borderland between history and myth.

With Riel and Tecumseh, Gutteridge finds two historical figures who indulge in conscious mythologizing. Riel cultivates tenaciously his self-images of prophet and messiah where Tecumseh's oratorical power, while asserting the catastrophe and pacifying powers of language, enlarges his own vision of a personal myth that will be both strong and liberating:

> I want to fashion good words forever, stretch my body
> into a continuous sentence, humiliate the air with speech,
> break the chronology of my people's despair, sew them
> green stories, chronicles of hope, weave a new history
> from our twin beginnings: we shall see our own shame
> and the white man his — he will smile and give up his
> books, his bellicose reading of the world's working-out,
> my myths will eat him, page by page, into silence —
> decoded, he will be free at last to utter those poems that
> have no need for the curvature of words. . . .

At the end, of course, Tecumseh becomes the spirit in all things, the historical hero, prophet, and mythopoet.

In sum, Gutteridge's tetralogy crystallizes his sympathy for underdogs, whether they exist in western society or outside it, sinister or disturbed. This produces, or all the sophisticated symbolism, a worldly vision of a human struggle for power. But this power is not simply the power of politics or technology. It is, instead, the power to evolve spiritually, and it is a mystery treated with sensitivity. Clearly, the heroes in Gutteridge's landscapes are not the bourgeois proponents of planning, technical efficiency, regimentation, and social convention. When his men become heroic, and it is always in extremis, they do so in circumstances that do not afford the protection of social order.

What this produces is a sentimentalization of the primitive ethos, and such an effect is yet another demonstration that the romantic age of Canadian poetry is not really over. From Purdy to Cohen, from Gutteridge to Atwood, there is still a fascination with masks, with gestures and expressions of the primitive, as if that element were the residue of a civilization purer than our own. All these poets are concerned with visions of destruction which may or may not be translated into a psyche-enlarging apocalypse, but the combination of brutal sex, physical violence, and psychic confusion is metaphysical in its attempt to yield a transcendental value as art. The danger inherent in this position, as Sandra Djwa has pointed out in a piece on Cohen's black romanticism, is "the temptation it offers to mistake catalogued sensation for new revelation." [7] I think, however, Gutteridge generally succeeds admirably in resisting this temptation.

Notes

1 – "The Documentary Poem: A Canadian Genre," in Contexts of Canadian Criticism, ed. Eli Mandel (Chicago: Univ. of Chicago Press, 1971), pp. 267-81.

2 – Joseph Kinsey Howard, Strange Empire (Toronto: Swan Publishing, 1965) , pp. 44-45.

3 – J. E. Cirlot, A Dictionary Of Symbols, trans. Jack Sage (New York: Philosophical Library, 1962) , p, 308.

4 – Ibid., p. 231.

5 – See Maurice Hodgson, "Initiation And Quest: Early Canadian Journals," Canadian Literature, No. 38 (Autumn 1968) , pp. 29-40.

6 – Northrop Frye, "Conclusion to a Literary History of Canada," in The Bush Garden (Toronto: Anansi, 1971), p. 232.

7 – Sandra Djwa, "Leonard Cohen : Black Romantic," in Poets and Critics, ed. George Woodcock (Toronto: Oxford Univ. tangerine is picked out of darkness.

Home Ground: Don Gutteridge's Literary Novels

by Kevin Spence

Donald Gutteridge was born on September 30, 1937 in Sarnia Ontario, and shortly after was brought back to Point Edward, where he would live out most of his childhood. It is from this stretch of his early life that Gutteridge draws much of his inspiration and the subject of eight novels. A poet, teacher and a professor, he published several works of verse before the first of his novels *Bus-Ride* was released in 1974. Since then, Gutteridge has authored two dozen works of fiction, creating a substantial body of work.

Writing Style

Don Gutteridge's writing style can best be described as accessible romanticism. He makes use of vivid imagery, poetic phrasing and incisive metaphor to lend emotional impact without the use of overly complex language or metaphor. Gutteridge's portfolio extends through a broad variety of settings and genres, including tragedy, comedy, historical, fantastical, or modern, offering something for most prospective readers. I would contend, however, that Don Gutteridge's novels are best read by those with an active interest in Canadian history and culture. Though a book like *The Perilous Journey of Gavin the Great* offers a witty take on a classic fable structure, the lion's share of Gutteridge's novels breathe life into the days of his boyhood in Point Edward. Gutteridge uses his life experience to explore a people, place and time through his own eyes. It is this unparalleled authenticity that makes Gutteridge's portrayals of his characters into something between fact and fiction, an immortalized recreation of the kind of people who once were. The Novels of Lambton County are an exercise in not just writing, but storytelling. Gutteridge shares pieces of himself and his origins through his prose.

Themes and Narrative

Whether ordinary or fantastical, Gutteridge uses three consistent themes and narrative tools in his books: coming of age, the importance of place, and the juxtaposition of innocence and harsh reality. Each work offers a unique perspective on what living and growing in Point Edward was like. Gutteridge's protagonists span both sexes, all ages and occupy over a century of history. There is also a look at the history of more marginalized groups around Point Edward in his largest novel, *Lily's Story*. Through the myriad perspectives involved, the Novels of Lambton County do not shy away from the darker side of its history. The inclusion of the less savoury elements of Canadian village life is connected to Gutteridge's use of juxtaposition. Even in the more comically intended novels of Gutteridge's earlier years, *Bus-Ride* and *All in Good Time,* there are ominous undertones. Through the eyes of boys and provincial village men, Gutteridge highlights not just the passing intolerance and suspicion, but the bleak insecurity of the future that frames their provincial hopes and dreams. A concise and self-contained example of this juxtaposition can be seen in Gutteridge's second novel, *All in Good Time*. In even the innocent context of a piano lesson, the reader cannot escape a reminder of their loss: "'Well, I did bring some Chopin.' He flushed, and again she was reminded of the innocence of his glance. What was she doing? Some field in France, this very moment, might be reclaiming the ripped flesh of her husband." (Gutteridge, 1980, 44) It is in this fashion that Gutteridge's dark sense of humour and tragedy remains ever-present in his novels.

Arguably the most primary theme within Don Gutteridge's novels is the importance of place. There is a single exception in the review section below, but seven of the eight novels covered in this essay are devoted to developing the history and importance of Lambton County. The villagers of The Point are inextricably linked to the land that surrounds them, both conjoining to create the "Village" as Gutteridge wants the reader to see it. The importance of place in his writing is more than a monument or frieze of his childhood, however. Gutteridge explicitly creates the Village as a microcosm of Canada.

A small piece of the gestalt that is the Canada he treasures, The Point serves as memory and metaphor, a tool to share the author's romanticized vision of his beloved childhood home and one used to explore a more universal conception of what connects Canadians. Gutteridge's tone as is that of a storyteller weaving a tale alongside the reader. His tone is one in a long Canadian tradition, both personal and largely informal, displayed prominently in his unorthodox use of pronouns. Stories about The Point, and about Canada are not from the perspective of a passive observer. Rather they are from within, providing the subjectivity that gives each novel its authentic character.

Overview and Analysis

An overview of the novelistic works of Don Gutteridge is best done in three sections: Pre-Point Edward Novels, the Novels of The Point, and the others. Both the Pre-Point Novels and the Novels of The Point feature their geographical location as a matter of chief importance. The themes and narrative through-line are as much about the development of the village itself as any of the individual characters. The Novels of The Point consist of four books: *Bus-Ride, All in Good Time, Summer's Idyll,* and *Winter's Descent.*. These books are the most sequential of Gutteridge's works, happening within roughly a decade from 1939 to the late 1940s and feature a recurring and interrelated set of characters. The Pre-Point Novels consist of two books, *How the World Began* and *Lily's Story*, a revised combination of two older works: *St. Vitus' Dance* and *Shaman's Ground.* These two books take place through from the mid-19th century to the early 20th century.

The greater part of these novels takes place before Point Edward exists. Thematically, the Pre-Point novels are distinguished by a generally bleak or tragic tone. They also concern themselves with the formation of Point Edward, Canada's railway and nationhood, and the Anishinaabe/Pottawatomie people in Gutteridge's novels. The novels of The Point are characterized by the setting of the already established village of Point Edward and a tighter time-period. The last two novels covered in this essay, *Bewilderment* and *The Perilous Adventures of Gavin the Great,* do not fit easily in themes or motifs of the other five novels, and ergo are better suited to individual analysis.

How the World Began is a novel following a gentle young farm-boy by the name of Ti-Luc. It begins in the year 1794 on a small farm in the largely unsettled Lambton county. The book follows Ti-Luc's idyllic childhood in the untamed bush of Canada, his transition to adulthood, and his exposure to the unkind realities of the world outside his isolated farm. His journey is inundated with themes of trauma, loss, and purpose. Of all Gutteridge's novels, *How the World Began* might have the bleakest overall tone. It opens with violence: a vengeful Pottawatomie attack on a farmstead as they retreat from the Battle of

Fallen Timbers. In one uncharacteristically violent stroke, Gutteridge introduces the reader to a very different Point Edward. He displays the historical unrest in the region, introduces Trill, Ti-Luc's adopted sister, and the parable of Carcajou and Wisakedjak, a recurring duology of First Nations god figures. Within the greater scope of the Lambton County novels, *How the World Began* serves as the prologue. It demonstrates the harshness of life before The Village through Ti-Luc's experience of war, privation, and disease. It is this series of traumas that Gutteridge uses to characterize the early Ontario community. Be it the shattering of tribal nations, the suffering of slaves, or the helplessness of a family succumbing to disease, the Pre-Point is Gutteridge's examination of cultural baggage, personal and societal. These larger traumas are paralleled by the personal ones experienced by Ti-Luc, interweaving individual and nation through tragedy. Narratively, it is through his small-scale experiences of Canada's national issues that Ti-Luc grows into adulthood and fatherhood. Chief among those coming at the hands of his brother Cal, who dreams of more than the small world beyond The Bend and enlists, finding engagement in the war of 1812. Gentle Ti-Luc, who wished for nothing beyond the borders of his farm-stead, goes out in search of his brother. Through his suffering on his journey, Ti-Luc is tempered into manhood, just as his brother is forced to face the reality of the war he had so lionized. The loss and hardship on the journey reaffirm the value of what he left behind. Ti-Luc's struggle is in the desperate wish to return to the normalcy of the past – having to cope with the tragic reality that it can never be the same, and forging on regardless.

Second in the Pre-Point books is *Lily's Story*, which follows the titular Lily Fairchild from 1845 into the early 1920s. There are two strong thematic narratives at play in *Lily's Story*. The personal story of Lily, which is concerned with loss and the will to overcome grief; and the story of Point Edward, for it is within the pages of *Lily's Story* that Gutteridge details the historical formation of the town. Through the eyes of Lily, the reader can see Point Edward grow from a river-junction shanty town into the modern village that features in later novels. *Lily's Story* can best be described as a sequence of tragic relationships. There are the personal losses of Lily herself, perpetually coming to love someone and finding them torn away by disease, war and old age. There are also the losses that serve as historical commentary on the dark past of Canada and the cost of progress. Lily, growing initially far from the more settled lands near Sarnia and London, offers insight into the lives of runaway slaves, the fading language and culture of the last free tribes, the present day Anishinaabe, and the plight of women without political agency. Just as Lily loses her loved ones, the novel details the losses of the marginalized and the down-trodden, a distinctive feature of the Pre-Point novels. In later writings, the village of Point Edward is relatively peaceful and its tragedies are few. *Lily's Story* is in some sense a monument to the loss of the people who came before. A dedication to the slaves and soldiers and Anishinaabe on whose graves the village was built. Lily's story parallels that motif. Lily, elderly and alone, experiences the final loss of her home, replaced by a literal monument for the losses of the Great War (Gutteridge 2014, 410-411)

Lily's Story is a tragedy, but one that urges an unshakeable optimism. Though she experiences incessant loss and grief, Lily always manages to find the strength and courage to move on. Her story is one of self-admitted suffering, but she explicitly endorses an optimistic philosophy. An indomitable will to keep loving despite the pain of grief:

"Cora, you've told me more about your life and travails than any one man ought to know, and I'll be damned if I can see where you had much choice. Like most women you've been devastated by wars you never started, diseases you can't cure, and children who die on you or run off to lead their own lives without a pennyworth of gratitude. The world cares only for the species, and women bear the brunt of that reality." Cora mulled that over for a while. "May be" she said. "But I chose somethin'. Every time." "And what would that be?" "I chose to love". (Gutteridge, 2014, 502)

Lily embraces the inevitability of loss and the pain that comes with it. In a sense, each of Lily's losses, and her life itself can be interpreted as a series of 'coming of age' tales. Lily has her life torn away by tragic circumstances, and rebuilds it. Lily always chooses to craft a new life, find new things and new people to value. It is a continuum from child to elder, constantly discovering new ways to be, even if it hurts her. Lily's journey is a cyclical one. An inverse of the second narrative through-line of The Point itself. The Village moves ever forward, and the memory of what it used to be fades, save for on the pages of Gutteridge's novels.

The Novels of The Point comprise most of Gutteridge's novelistic works and share many common characteristics. Each book follows a single point of view in the late 1930s or 1940s, features a coming-of-age narrative, and explores how a village reflects the nation. Gutteridge uses perspectives of all different ages and ambitions to depict his vision of The Village, one where the reeve is also a garbage man, there is a single pub, and veterans of the war can live in quiet reprieve. The cast that Gutteridge portrays are emblematic of his broader view, where no matter how fractious or petty they can seem, the villagers adhere to a common sentiment and feeling. In portraying this unified spirit, Gutteridge also makes an explicit connection to the nation. The spirit of the village is reflective of the people, to be identified together.

In *Bus-Ride*, Gutteridge draws on The Point's love of hockey to portray the spirit of the village as representative of the nation:

"'Hello Canada, and hockey fans in the United States!' They, like a million others on this night in March of 1939, would be content to listen, to focus all senses on a single voice, riding outward to the far stretches of the land, carrying in its rhythms and intonations the legends of its generation." (Gutteridge, 2019, 67)

The radio play-by- play serves as a literal and metaphorical device connecting Canadians, framing Point Edward as a single piece in a mosaic. It is through the singular will of the village that Gutteridge turns the individual characters, and by extension each individual Canadian, into the fabric of the whole.

The wreath-laying ceremony in *All in Good Time* is another symbolic and metaphorical connection. A demonstration of a common will for the patchwork villagers: "Many wept, quietly. Others stood, feeling nothing but the awesomeness of the moment as if time itself had stopped to enclose them all in the stunning fusion of a second borrowed from eternity." (Gutteridge, 1980, 159) This theme of commonality, owing to its metaphorical nature, is expressed in a similar manner across the Novels of The Point.

Coming of age, though it is featured in each individual Novel of The Point, is expressed differently each time. There are four separate coming-of-age narratives at play: boyhood identity, sexual awakening, manhood, and middle-aged reinvigoration. The first and youngest stages of this 'coming of age' spectrum are in *Summer's Idyll* and *Winter's Descent.* Gutteridge's only direct prequel/sequel, both follow the protagonist, young Will, through two important transitions in his life. *Summer's Idyll* chronicles Will as he transitions from early childhood into his adolescent years through a journey of self-discovery. The nominal story is about Will and his friends putting on a circus-esque show for their school, while the meta-narrative has the boy experiencing and losing some of his youthful wonder. *Summer's Idyll* has Will come of age through abandoning comforting childhood illusions and fantasies.

Gutteridge does so by playing with appearance and reality through several sub-plots: the mysterious 'stranger,' more mundane than Will's childish imagination conjures up, the failure of his parents' marriage, and the subtly-communicated costs of war.

A direct sequel to *Summer's Idyll*, *Winter's Descent* has Will flourishing into youthful manhood. Where *Summer's Idyll* has Will growing past childhood whimsy to see the world for how it really is, *Winter's Descent* is his venture into that world. *Winter's Descent* is a coming of age centered around desire. Will breaks free from his shell with a newfound discovery of love, the opposite sex, and his passion for writing and reading. In embodying his desires, Will undergoes a metamorphosis, defining himself from his peers, who had constituted such an important element of his identity in *Summer's Idyll.*

Bus-Ride is the story of young Will and his transition into independent manhood. It is defined not by soft romantic discovery or self-identity, but by struggle. Bill Underhill is in constant turmoil, stuck between the mountainous expectations of the entire Village and his own unclear future. The villagers view him as their star hockey hopeful, but Bill isn't even certain he wants to play hockey (*Bus-Ride*, 2019, 18). Part of Bill's indecision comes from his powerful resentment for the constrictive, quiet life that Point Edward provides. Bill envies his father, who not only saw the world, but had "Been in the world" (*Bus-Ride*, 2019, 94) and a part of its history. Bill's journey forces him to consider his future and his freedom. In trying to find his way out of the Point, Bill considers what the village means to him as he passes into manhood and confronts an impossible decision at the outbreak of the Second World War.

All in Good Time, following Horace Macintosh, The Point's Reeve (and garbage truck driver), toys with the meaning of a coming-of-age story. Not a boy passing into manhood, the Reeve's coming of age is rather a reinvigoration. As a result of the ups and downs of his going for an ill-considered political gamble, the Reeve discovers new passions and a new purpose, decades past his boyhood. Horace, so unlike Will or Bill, is ambitious and pretentious, but learns to discard old prejudices, make himself anew, and learn to love the old again.

Bewilderment: A Novel of the Great Depression takes place in Point Edward in 1936, but shares few themes with the other Novels of The Point. As a book, *Bewilderment* is a fictionalized history. It is a means of immortalizing the everyday suffering and loss that working class people went through in a period of duress. The story follows the well-intentioned coal worker Gabe Goodfellow as he helps put on a carnival and collect bond money during the height of the Great Depression, all the while trying to care for his own family. *Bewilderment's* aim and achievement is to capture the emotional aspect of history. To see hardship and privation through Gabe's eyes and to humanize what is a matter of historical canon. The tone and themes of *Bewilderment* serve as an absurdist juxtaposition, each page filled with detail on the fallout of economic disaster, clashing against the hope and marvelous excess of a Carnival. Gutteridge reaffirms the struggle that working class families experienced in the depression, and simultaneously the reason for it. In the midst of his hardships and moral compromises, Gabe still finds love and helps bring the village together in wonder at the spectacle of the carnival. More than any of Gutteridge's other works, *Bewilderment* is beholden to its title, providing a window into the inner lives of those living in Point Edward during the Great Depression.

The Perilous Journey of Gavin the Great is Gutteridge's greatest departure from his previous works, being a foray into the genre of fantasy. In the tradition of classic fables, *The Perilous Journey of Gavin the Great* is both whimsical and dark. Set in the forest called Earthwood, it is a world populated by talking and anthropomorphized forest creatures. It follows the story of Gavin, a raccoon, and his two siblings as they flee from a great disaster that threatens to destroy the entirety of their forest home. Thematically, *The Perilous Journey* flirts with biblical allegory, featuring apocalyptic floods, a life-saving and animal-laden raft, and archetypal figures like the wily fox. It is unlike any of Gutteridge's other works in that it has no readily apparent thematic metaphors. Rather, the themes of *The Perilous Journey* are reflective of classical fables and the hero's journey. Gavin and his companions face danger and fear in a grand adventure and must triumph through their cleverness, courage and virtue. Perhaps most remarkable about *The Perilous Journey* is the tone. It combines light-hearted parody and grim danger effortlessly. One moment Gutteridge might humorously draw a comparison to the Arthurian canon when Gavin acquires a "sword" he refers to as Hex-Calibre – in reality a man's discarded hunting knife (*Gavin the Great*, 2012, 252), and in the next he might be describing the simultaneously comical and chilling beasts known as "Squeezels." Gavin's journey exists somewhere in the space of satire and genuine love for fairy-tale stories, with Gutteridge working self-aware mockery into a sincerely told story.

Conclusion

Don Gutteridge's writing, entirely separated from its cultural context, is valuable as a wholly authentic experience. He lived in the land so meticulously and lovingly crafted it into his novels. One can to this day wander the very haunts Gutteridge has written about, and walk in the footsteps of Will, Bill, or Lily. There is a timelessness to the works of Don Gutteridge even as they capture a piece of history.

Bibliography

Gutteridge, D. (1980). *All in Good Time*. Black Moss Press, Windsor.

Gutteridge, D. (1991). *How the World Began*. Moonstone Press, Goderich.

Gutteridge, D. (1993). *Summer's Idyll*. Oberon Press, Ottawa.

Gutteridge, D. (1996). *Winter's Descent*. Oberon Press, Ottawa.

Gutteridge, D. (2000). *Bewilderment*. Borealis Press Ottawa..

Gutteridge, D. (2010). *The Perilous Adventures of Gavin the Great*. Borealis Press, Ottawa.

Gutteridge, D. (2014). *Lily's Story*. Bev Editions. Toronto.

Gutteridge, D. (2019). *Bus Ride*. Bev Editions. Toronto.

Powell, R. (1974, June). Bus-Ride, Don Gutteridge: *Quill & Quire*.

Don Gutteridge was born in Sarnia and raised in the nearby village of Point Edward. He taught High School English for seven years, later becoming a Professor in the Faculty of Education at Western University, where he is now Professor Emeritus. He is the author of more than seventy books: poetry, fiction and scholarly works in pedagogical theory and practice. He has published twenty-two novels, including the twelve-volume Marc Edwards mystery series, and forty books of poetry, one of which, Coppermine, was short-listed for the 1973 Governor-General's Award. In 1970 he won the UWO President's Medal for the best periodical poem of that year, "Death at Quebec." Don lives in London, Ontario.

Email: dongutteridge37@gmail.com.

CanLit Revealed

A Series of Review and Essay Books on Canadian Literature.

Here are two other QuodSermo books about <u>Don Gutteridge</u>

Title: *Five Canadian Poets: Analytical Essays on, James Deahl, John B. Lee,* ***Don Gutteridge****, Glen Sorestad, A. F. Moritz*
Author: M.Sc. Miguel Ángel Olivé Iglesias

ISBN – 9781989786369 (softcover)
ISBN – 9781989786376 (ebook)

Publisher: QuodSermo Publishing

Here you will find outstanding essays on both the biographical history as well as the literary history of five of Canada's top poets. This collection of essays brings literary life to Canadian poetry in the making. Examples of each poet's work are critiqued, examined and observed gently and sympathetically. They have been described as "well-researched love letters to poetry and the poetic spirit." These essays will open your eyes to poetry.

Title: *The Canadian Poet Who Wrote Himself Whole: Revealing the Poetics of* ***Don Gutteridge***
Author: M.Sc. Miguel Ángel Olivé Iglesias

ISBN – 978-1-989786-57-4 (softcover)
ISBN – 978-1-989786-58-1 (ebook)

Publisher: QuodSermo Publishing

The Canadian Poet Who Wrote Himself Whole is a fine collection of essays and reviews by scholar and essayist Miguel Ángel Olivé Iglesias on the poetry and prose of world class Canadian poet Don Gutteridge.

www.ingramcontent.com/pod-product-compliance
Lightning Source LLC
Chambersburg PA
CBHW080337030726
47594CB00011B/4064

* 9 7 8 1 9 8 9 7 8 6 5 9 8 *